Budtender's Blueprint®

Compassion and Chemistry at the Cannabis Counter

Mission Point Press

2554 Chandler Road
Traverse City, Michigan 49696
www.MissionPointPress.com
231-421-9513

Design by Mark Pate

Printed in the United States of America

ISBN: 978-1-965278-96-3
Library of Congress Control Number: 2025914169

Budtender's Blueprint®

Compassion and Chemistry at the Cannabis Counter

Angie Roullier

M·P·P
www.MissionPointPress.com

For Chloe, who reminded me how much mental, physical and emotional energy is involved in this labor of love for this plant. I hope your free spirit knows that you will always have a home within our culture.

"I only wish I had this as a reference a decade ago when I was just starting out in the industry and was continuously searching terms on Google just to keep up in conversations. This is a tremendous resource for business owners, budtenders, lawyers, consultants, and policymakers, and will definitely have a permanent place on my desk from now on."

Douglas Mains
Government Relations, Regulatory, and Administrative Law Attorney

"Angie is incredibly knowledgeable and passionate about helping others, but I'm willing to bet you already know that! Recommending Angie goes beyond endorsing her as a cannabis expert; it is a testament to her compassionate approach to education and unwavering dedication to safety and accessibility for patients everywhere."

Raven Ariola, M.S.
Program Director of Cannabis and Medicinal Plant Science at Beal University

"I worked closely with Angie during the grand opening of Oakland County's first Provisioning Center. Its success is the direct result of her dedication and passion for the patients. Angie's persistent focus on patient safety and education sets her apart from the profit-driven businesses that dominate the market. She is the first person in the know on new discoveries in the field, always up-to-date on this ever-changing industry. As a patient, I would be hard-pressed to find a more compassionate and knowledgeable caregiver. As a colleague, her professionalism and mission-oriented drive are second to none."

Ryan Schuler
Corpsman Veteran

CONTENTS

INTRODUCTION

Why did I decide to pull large chunks from my first book, *Pot for the People* to craft this manuscript specifically targeted at cannabis retail workers? To be honest, most of you are doing it wrong. And I don't believe the blame falls on you as individuals. The blame lies with those who own the roof you work under. The vast majority of owners do not care whether their staff, or their consumers, for that matter, are educated—so long as the dough keeps rolling in. When it comes to cannabis retail training, it seems to only cover point-of-sale systems, local laws to avoid fines, and how to sell their highest-paid sponsor's product. This approach to cannabis is, quite frankly, not only hurting the consumer but also killing our culture one sale at a time.

Most budtenders I have come across are genuinely interested in learning more about how the plant works, what products (not brands) work best for specific afflictions, and why there is a difference in how you can take it. For those of you who simply don't care one way or the other, may I suggest you move to the back of the house or find a different line of work within the industry?

In the following pages, you will find all kinds of cited research that backs up my knowledge on the chemicals in the plant, the different methods of intake, how to successfully interact with consumers, and how to handle policy situations as they arise. Now, who in the hell do I think I am to give such advice? Because I spent almost a decade where you are. I have suffered the uncalled-for constant rush on a Tuesday. I have been bored to tears on those painfully slow Saturdays (honestly, how much cleaning can you do?). I have been that manager who showed up on a vendor day morning with the vendor's product still not on site. I know your sore feet, your frustrations with the powers that pull the strings, and the "people are the worst" situations. No two days are the same when you work the cannabis counter, which was one of my favorite things about my time spent in cannabis retail. As refreshing as it was, some days it seemed like an endless supply of pops to the chops. Cannabis retail is not for the weak, but I promise it is beyond rewarding for those who prevail.

So why do we do it? Lord knows it's not the money. I personally did it for selfish reasons. It makes me feel good to help people with this plant. It was a buzz all on its own when a patient would return with words of gratitude or a thankful hug for the guidance on the path that led to some relief. I still am, and always will be, in this industry for the patient. My hope for those of you already in the industry is that you may find different approaches to customer care or recognize a bad habit to break. If you are new to cannabis retail, I hope these pages help you build solid foundations based on science and compassion.

DISCLAIMER

We have only just begun the journey to fully understand the natural chemicals of cannabis and the promise they may hold as plant-based medicine. Just thinking about not only the different independent compounds but also the endless combinations of these compounds, quite frankly makes my head hurt. Thankfully, there are those out there who have a true passion for such tasks and take it as far as they can on a daily basis.

As I will state several times throughout these pages, these are the very, very bare bones of what we know so far. And I am sure that there is an abundance of scientists and scholars alike who will say that I haven't explained the plant (or its effects) to its fullest extent. Of course, I haven't. I am not a scientist, and even they don't know all there is to know about the matter.

I want you to think of the following terms, definitions, and examples as if I were a senior in high school tutoring a fifth grader in English for the purpose of understanding verbs, adjectives, and proper nouns. Again, these are the bare bones as we currently know them.

PLANT

HEMP VS. MARIJUANA

We have all heard both terms when referencing cannabis, but what exactly is the difference between the two? Both come from Cannabis sativa L., but what separates them is partly genetics, and partly a matter of the law of the land. Let's start with genetics. According to the Hash Museum, "Cannabis" is the name given to the plant itself. "Sativa" simply means "sown" and is used to indicate the common or cultivated form of the plant. The "L" refers to Carolus Linnaeus, the Swedish botanist who first gave this common yet celebrated herb its scientific classification in 1753.

Since then, two more main types of cannabis have been identified: Cannabis indica was classified in 1785 and Cannabis ruderalis in 1924. Both are subspecies of the Cannabis sativa family, and the three types are distinguished by the different characteristics and traits they display."[1]

Think along the lines of the tomato plant. You can have Cherry, Roma, or Heirloom tomatoes. They are each different in size, acidity, and consistency, but at the end of the day, they are all still tomatoes.

Sativa   Indica   Ruderalis

Hemp is generally bred for its industrial use in fiber, fuel, and food, while marijuana is grown for the medicinal value of its cannabinoids. Since the Farm Bill of 2018, the definition is that any cannabis plant that has more than 0.3% of THC is considered to be marijuana, and anything less is hemp. Imagine you are a hemp farmer that sells their harvest for fiber in the clothing industry, but for whatever reason the crop tests at 0.7% THC. This farmer now has acres of very illegal marijuana, and some very big problems.

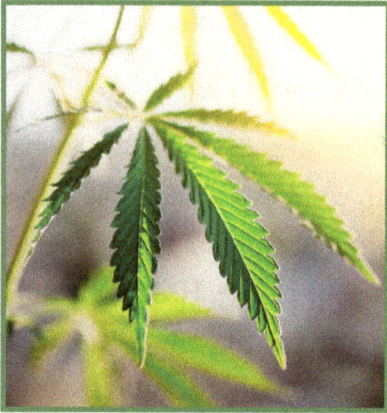

It turns out that cannabis is a superhero before it even leaves the dirt.

Cannabis is a bioaccumulator by nature. In fact, it is a hyperaccumulator, along with sunflowers and mustard plants. Cannabis has the capacity to absorb metals and other toxins from soil by drinking them in through their roots, where they are then moved and stored in its stems and leaves.

One of my favorite examples of this was an Italian sheep farmer who discovered in 2008 that his land had been poisoned by dioxin, a toxic chemical that is extremely difficult to break down once it is in the environment. Dioxin can cause cancer, reproductive and developmental problems, damage to the immune system, and can interfere with hormones.[2]

This toxin, known to be stored in the fatty tissue of animals, had been leaking from a large steel plant in the area, prompting the Italian government to test this farmer's livestock for the contaminant. When the tests came back positive, he was forced to slaughter his entire herd of 600 sheep.

Not willing to give up on his land, the farmer decided to plant hemp for its bioaccumulating abilities, hoping it would save his farm. Not only would the hemp rid his part of the planet of toxins in the dirt, but the garbage-grabbing crop could also be burned later as biofuel. Although time-consuming, this method can provide a natural fuel source.[3]

But buyer beware, as this fact warrants caution. Yes, it's very cool that this plant can clean the dirt, but think about all of those toxins contained within a plant that may end up being harvested for human consumption (CBD). If the processor isn't careful, the heavy metals could (and sometimes do) make their way into that CBD tincture or gummy you're so fond of. Always check the test results, better known as a COA (certificate of analysis), for any heavy metals.

On a positive note, I have heard of many farmers who plant hemp for the first couple of seasons to clean their own land and then have the plants destroyed. After a few rounds of hemp, their dirt is squeaky clean, and they can plant with the confidence of a clean end product.

THE HEMP WARS

I find it utterly ridiculous that we are squabbling amongst ourselves when it comes to the compounds in the cannabis plant. That being said, I will put up a fight against the "franken-noids" being produced—mostly on the hemp side of things—just to make a buck. With well over 100 different compounds naturally occurring in the plant, I see no reason to create new ones—potentially harmful ones—until we can figure out what the originals can do.

Just a few issues that are bringing people to fisticuffs is the loophole in the Farm Bill of 2018, which allows for the sale and transport of hemp products across our great 50 states, as long as they are under the 0.3% THC threshold. Those in regulated market states are upset that they have been raked over the coals, sometimes spending millions of dollars to get their hands on a state-sanctioned license, while those in the hemp market pay pennies in comparison to setting up shop—and admittedly take some business away from the regulated market.

I also feel for those in states that only have hemp products to choose from when looking to use cannabis as medicine. The regulations on how these products are made are not anywhere near as strict as those in regulated states, which increases the odds of you purchasing some shady stuff. But I will say that I do embrace certain products from hemp suppliers, as they are the only ones to carry a wide variety of minor cannabinoids for those not wanting to catch a buzz.

Then there is the argument of the "franken-noids" that I had mentioned. The problem, as I see it, is that these are made in a lab and if they do show up in their natural form, it's in really, really small amounts which cannot be produced in the volume required for consumer consumption. So, what do they do? They take a natural cannabinoid and dicker with it in the lab, creating a new chemical and call it cannabis. First, passing it off as a natural substance is an irresponsible joke. Second, the process that the mad scientist uses in creating these chemical conversions is questionable at best. What chemicals are they using? How much of said chemical is left behind that the consumer is putting into their bodies? If you thought we knew not so much about the cannabis plant coming right out of the ground, you can guess how much less we know about the long-term effects of these man-made synthetics. I'm not a fan.

I find the whole thing to be a double-edged sword. Those of us who care for the plant, and the people, want it to be safe and accessible to anyone and everyone interested in botanical-based medicine. But is access only through gas station and quasi-safety parameters better than having no access at all?

Not to mention, if you are one of those "If you can't buy it the way we have to sell it, you shouldn't be allowed to have it at all," you may want to check in and see where your compassion is at for those suffering.

CANNABINOIDS

By definition, "Cannabinoids, broadly speaking, are a class of biological compounds that bind to cannabinoid receptors. They are most frequently sourced from and associated with the plants of the Cannabis genus, including Cannabis sativa, Cannabis indica, and Cannabis ruderalis."[4]

Cannabinoids come in these three forms:

- **Phytocannabinoids – Produced by the plant**
- **Endocannabinoids – Produced naturally by your body**
- **Synthetic Cannabinoids – Man-made**

KNOW YOUR CANNABINOIDS
how can cannabinoids benefit you?

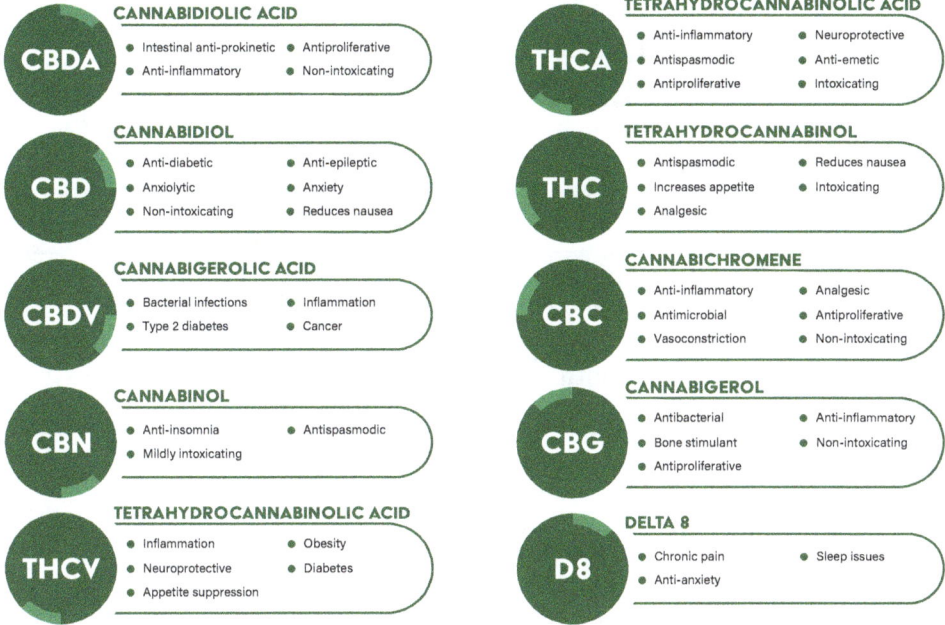

CBDA — CANNABIDIOLIC ACID
- Intestinal anti-prokinetic
- Anti-inflammatory
- Antiproliferative
- Non-intoxicating

CBD — CANNABIDIOL
- Anti-diabetic
- Anxiolytic
- Non-intoxicating
- Anti-epileptic
- Anxiety
- Reduces nausea

CBDV — CANNABIGEROLIC ACID
- Bacterial infections
- Type 2 diabetes
- Inflammation
- Cancer

CBN — CANNABINOL
- Anti-insomnia
- Mildly intoxicating
- Antispasmodic

THCV — TETRAHYDROCANNABINOLIC ACID
- Inflammation
- Neuroprotective
- Appetite suppression
- Obesity
- Diabetes

THCA — TETRAHYDROCANNABINOLIC ACID
- Anti-inflammatory
- Antispasmodic
- Antiproliferative
- Neuroprotective
- Anti-emetic
- Intoxicating

THC — TETRAHYDROCANNABINOL
- Antispasmodic
- Increases appetite
- Analgesic
- Reduces nausea
- Intoxicating

CBC — CANNABICHROMENE
- Anti-inflammatory
- Antimicrobial
- Vasoconstriction
- Analgesic
- Antiproliferative
- Non-intoxicating

CBG — CANNABIGEROL
- Antibacterial
- Bone stimulant
- Antiproliferative
- Anti-inflammatory
- Non-intoxicating

D8 — DELTA 8
- Chronic pain
- Anti-anxiety
- Sleep issues

THC and CBD are considered to be "major" cannabinoids, while other cannabinoids are considered "minor" or "rare" due to their low concentrations found in the plant. But much like the Cusack siblings, I believe that they are not getting the credit they deserve. Just because these cannabinoids are less abundant does not mean that they don't have their own roles to play.

(Since I struggle with saying the names of some of these cannabinoids, I have taken it upon myself to do my best in spelling out the pronunciations of the overly large and intimidating words.) Let's take a look at the top ten cannabinoids and their pros and cons.

THC stands for Tetrahydrocannabinol (tetra-hydro-ka-nab-a-nall). It is intoxicating and can also be referred to as Delta 9 or D9. This is the cannabinoid that is notorious for the "high" people can feel when using cannabis.

My goodness, how so many people get all wound up over these three little letters. But THC, in moderation, is not such a bad guy after all. He's just misunderstood and often misused.

POTENTIAL BENEFICIAL EFFECTS OF THC

1 CHRONIC PAIN   2 GLAUCOMA   3 MUSCLE SPASTICITY

4 LOW APPETITE   5 NAUSEA ISSUES   6 SLEEP ISSUES

THC also comes with both good and bad side effects. The undesirable ones can be overwhelming and even downright dangerous if a person consumes too much.[5]

POTENTIAL NEGATIVE EFFECTS OF THC

1 COORDINATION PROBLEMS   2 DELAYED REACTION TIMES   3 DRY MOUTH

4 ANXIETY   5 DRY/RED EYES   6 MEMORY LOSS

7 INTOXICATION   8 INCREASED HEART RATE

The cannabis plant does not make THC, but rather THCA, and it is up to humans and/or time to change it.

THCA stands for Tetrahydrocannabinolic Acid (tetra-hydro-ka-nab-in-o-lick). It is nonintoxicating and serves as the precursor to the ever-popular THC. So, in English, if you were to pluck a fresh bud from a flowering cannabis plant and pop it into your mouth, THCA is what you would get (among other things). Adding raw cannabis to your diet is becoming more popular, and I have to say—I am a big admirer. For me, THCA feels like getting a shot of B12.

Now, if you hit the same bud with heat, you'll knock off the "A" (acid form), leaving you with the intoxicating THC that we all know. This is called decarboxylation—or decarbing for short. We will get into what temperatures at which different cannabinoids convert and/or cook off at later on. But until then, let's focus on what this nonintoxicating acid form of THC can do before you spark it.[6]

POTENTIAL BENEFICIAL EFFECTS OF THCA

1 INFLAMMATION   **2** EPILEPSY

POTENTIAL NEGATIVE EFFECTS OF THCA

1 JITTERS   **2** LACK OF SLEEP

3 CAN BE UNSTABLE DUE TO CONVERSION

What is the deal with THCA flower?

As I mentioned when speaking about the hemp wars, there is a ton of misinformation running around the loophole. A big part of the problem is that the powers that be don't understand the compounds they are regulating. THCA flower is a perfect example of this confusion.

In states where only hemp products are legal, you will find a long laundry list of THCA products, including everything from gummies to concentrates. While gummies will have little change as they pass through your system, anything that requires heat to consume is a completely different story.

Let's say you take a joint of "THCA flower" from South Carolina and a regular joint from a dispensary in Michigan's adult-use market. Both certificates of analysis (COAs) state that they contain 25% THCA. Once either of the joints are set on fire the heat will convert it, dropping the acid form and leaving you with THC. In other words, the two joints are exactly the same. All flower in its natural state is primarily THCA, regardless of where it was purchased. The same holds true for concentrates—whether it's dabs or hash, as it sits in the package it is mostly THCA, until of course you take a flame to it. Those passing restrictions on THC while allowing THCA either have zero clue about the chemicals they're regulating or—in the words of Tom Petty—"whatever you know, just play dumb."

CBD stands for Cannabidiol (canna-bid-dial). It is nonintoxicating and is the second most popular cannabinoid found in the cannabis plant. It is well known for offering therapeutic properties without the "high" that her big sister, THC, produces. The World Health Organization (WHO) reports: "In humans, CBD exhibits no effects indicative of any abuse or dependence potential ... To date, there is no evidence of public health related problems associated with the use of pure CBD."[7]

POTENTIAL BENEFICIAL EFFECTS OF CBD

1 ANXIETY	2 CHRONIC PAIN	3 INFLAMMATION
4 SLEEP ISSUES	5 ADDICTION	

This cannabinoid seems to be everywhere and promises to do everything—but that is not the case. CBD should be treated like any other drug and requires your due diligence when considering it as a form of medicine.

POTENTIAL NEGATIVE EFFECTS OF CBD

1 DRY MOUTH	2 DRUG INTERACTIONS
3 DIARRHEA	4 SLEEP ISSUES

Let's talk about the term "nonpsychoactive," and how it relates to cannabis.

This always reminds me of the words of Inigo Montoya, "You keep using that word; I do not think it means what you think it means."

This term seems to be plastered everywhere from your local CBD shop to research papers to induce a feeling of consumer security and a harmless alternative to pharmaceuticals. It is meant to ease our minds that the compound and/or the product will not get us high. Although CBD and the other "nonpsychoactive" cannabinoids will not get you stoned in the traditional sense of the word, it is definitely influencing your brain.

By definition, psychoactive is "Possessing the ability to alter mood, anxiety, behavior, cognitive process or mental tension ..."[8]

So therefore, caffeine and nicotine are a couple of other substances that are also considered to be psychoactive, yet these effects don't translate into being "stoned," as society sees it. And let's not forget the naturally occurring runner's high.

Those of us who are into the medical/science side of the cannabis industry prefer the more accurate term of "nonintoxicating." This verbiage sets a very clear distinction, not only between catching a buzz or not, but the effects it has on our brains as well.

CBDA, which stands for Cannabidiolic Acid (canna-bid-all-lick), is nonintoxicating and is considered to be a minor cannabinoid, having been first isolated in 1955. Just as THCA is the precursor to THC, CBDA is the precursor to CBD. It requires heat to drop the "A" and change the compound and its effects. CBDA + heat = CBD.

This little beauty has been shown to be 1000x more potent in reducing nausea than CBD and seems to play well with the other cannabinoids by enhancing their benefits.[9]

POTENTIAL BENEFICIAL EFFECTS OF CBDA

1 SEROTONIN REGULATION   **2** INFLAMMATION   **3** SEIZURE AID

POTENTIAL NEGATIVE EFFECTS OF CBDA

1 GUT DISRUPTION   **2** HEADACHES

3 CAN BE UNSTABLE DUE TO CONVERSION

CBN stands for Cannabinol (canna-bee-nall), is semi-intoxicating, and was initially isolated from Indian hemp in 1896, which made it the very first phytocannabinoid to be identified in cannabis. CBN is not made by the plant itself but is the end result of THC that has been degraded.

In plain English, this means that when your weed is exposed to air and light/heat over time, it turns into a completely new compound with different effects than the THC you started with.[10]

You will see more and more companies claim that CBN is the go-to for sleep, but the research is really scarce.[11]

There is, however, more evidence piling up about some other great benefits.

POTENTIAL BENEFICIAL EFFECTS OF CBN

1 CHRONIC PAIN   **2** APPETITE   **3** INFLAMMATION

4 FIBROMYALGIA   **5** IMMUNE HEALTH

POTENTIAL NEGATIVE EFFECTS OF CBN

1 INTOXICATION **2** APPETITE STIMULANT **3** LACK OF SLEEP

CBC stands for Cannabichromene (canna-bicker-mean), is nonintoxicating and is one of the most plentiful minor cannabinoids found in cannabis. In the 1980s, the anti-inflammatory effects of CBC were shown to be more effective than nonsteroidal anti-inflammatory drugs (NSAIDs), such as ibuprofen or aspirin.

Like some of the other interactive behaviors of cannabinoids, CBC works better as an anti-inflammatory when mixed with THC than when either cannabinoid is used alone.[12]

POTENTIAL BENEFICIAL EFFECTS OF CBC

1 MIGRAINES **2** BONE STRENGTH **3** INFLAMMATION

4 NEUROPROTECTION **5** TUMORS

POTENTIAL NEGATIVE EFFECTS OF CBC

1 DRY MOUTH

CBGA stands for Cannabigerolic Acid (canna-bige-er-o-lick), is nonintoxicating, and is considered to be the mother of all cannabinoids, as it is the precursor to THCA, CBDA, and CBCA.[13] Since the acid form will naturally decarb (convert) over time, it is rare to find CBGA concentrations in fully grown cannabis plants.[14] Imagine plucking an unripe green tomato. This is the stage, in a cannabis plant, where you will find CBGA. If you leave it be and let it continue to mature, the once-CBGA will have converted to THCA by the time you are ready to harvest.

POTENTIAL BENEFICIAL EFFECTS OF CBGA

1 INFLAMMATION   **2** CANCER

3 BACTERIAL INFECTIONS   **4** TYPE 2 DIABETES

POTENTIAL NEGATIVE EFFECTS OF CBGA

1 TIREDNESS   **2** DIARRHEA   **3** CHANGES IN APPETITE

CBG stands for Cannabigerol (canna-bidge-err-all), is nonintoxicating, and is the precursor to THC and CBD. Those with cancer often experience a lack of appetite, but CBG offers an alternative to the buzz-inducing effects of THC by also stimulating hunger which results in an increase of food ingested.

Not surprisingly, CBG taken in whole plant preparations was found to be more effective than the isolated form of CBG.[15]

POTENTIAL BENEFICIAL EFFECTS OF CBG

1 INFLAMMATION   **2** NEUROPROTECTANT   **3** APPETITE

*** There wasn't any sound research to warrant listing the negatives of CBG.***

THCV, or Tetrahydrocannabivarin (tetra-hydro-ka-nab-a-varin), is a semi-intoxicating cannabinoid, and comes from cannabigerovarinic acid (CBGVA), which is one of the two original minor cannabinoids. At this point it is THCVA, and we now know what happens to the "A" acid form when exposed to heat and/or light.[16]

THCV is found in very low concentrations in cannabis flowers, although breeders are working on making this minor cannabinoid more available.

POTENTIAL BENEFICIAL EFFECTS OF THCV

1 INFLAMMATION 2 OBESITY 3 DIABETES

4 NEUROPROTECTION 5 APPETITE SUPPRESSION

*** There wasn't any sound research to warrant listing the negatives of THCV.***

Delta 8 or D8 stands for Delta-8 tetrahydrocannabinol (tetra-hydro-ka-nab-a-nall), is intoxicating, and is a really close relative of D9 THC. The buzz can mimic that of THC, but on a more mellow level.[17]

Delta 8 is only found naturally in really, really low concentrations, so the majority of it is synthetically produced from a chemical conversion of CBD, usually from hemp.[18] My concern with this is that you really have to question the methods of those producing this chemically made cannabinoid, as it is mostly unregulated. The Farm Bill of 2018 gave them the loophole to sell it just about anywhere, but some states have required D8 to only be sold under their state-sanctioned medical marijuana programs. In my opinion, I believe this is the right call, as the state required testing protocols are very much needed to keep these producers honest, and the product clean.

POTENTIAL BENEFICIAL EFFECTS OF DELTA 8

1 CHRONIC PAIN 2 ANTI-ANXIETY 3 SLEEP ISSUES

POTENTIAL NEGATIVE EFFECTS OF DELTA 8

1 DRY MOUTH 2 PARANOIA 3 RED EYES

4 INCREASED HUNGER 5 SLEEP ISSUES

A few years back, I visited a licensed processor in Oklahoma to see how they were manufacturing Delta 8, as it was very new to the cannabis industry. The last leg of the tour put us in the kitchen where their D8 gummies were being laid out prior to packaging. The chef offered us a sample of the gummies stating that they were 10 mg each. At the time, the extent of my knowledge was that D8 felt like a 1:1 in that it was a lower key high. But knowing that I don't do well with edibles, and that I am rarely high in public, I bit the small candy in half and tossed the other half when no one was looking (stoners still judge).

Our tour wrapped up and we all headed out to lunch. I'm about halfway through my sandwich, and I realize that I am stoned out of my gourd! I did my best to maintain my composure throughout the rest of the meal but was thankful when the cold air in the parking lot hit my face. We returned to the facility, and once I was able to get my boss alone, I asked, "Are you high? I'm so high right now. I don't understand it. I only ate half!" The woman replied with, "I thought it was just me! What in the hell were in those things?" Not being as passive as I was, she flat out asked the chef if he was absolutely sure they were only 10 mgs. And then the room began to chuckle at our expense.

"Pretty sure, but we're still working on it. That's the fun of R&D, isn't it? Ha-ha. You should've seen Jason when we slipped him 500 mgs. Hee-hee. Smacked his head pretty good on a coffee table. Ha-ha. Show them the scar Jason. Ha-ha." I was beyond livid that we had been roofied, and no longer saw them as professionals, but knuckle-dragging snails and puppy dog tails.

Usually, I only have to stick my hand in the fire once to know that it will burn me, so I chalked this up as a teaching moment about the chemical conversions of synthetic cannabinoids.

CHEMOTYPES, PHENOTYPES & GENOTYPES ... OH MY!

I have to mention the distinction between these three terms, so as not to upset my plant science peeps, and also to lay the groundwork for our collective hopes in changing the way we identify marijuana. You will find that I defer to a few people in this book who are experts in the fields that I still cannot confidently grasp enough to teach. Chemotypes, phenotypes, and genotypes are a few such categories, and Josh Ferla is one such expert.

It was during the hazy, marijuana-filled summer days of the '80s in California's redwood engulfed Bay Area that Josh found his natural affinity for plants. His fascination with the appearances, the smells, and the other characteristics of the cannabis plant turned Josh into a second-generation cannabis grower. Reagan years be damned, he experimented with friends and family, trying different cultivation methods and techniques. Once out on his own, he dove into the science of indoor cultivation and the chemistry of cannabis cultivation to dial in his craft.

After a few years of fine tuning his talent by working on cannabis farms and in dispensaries, Josh got into commercial-scale farming at the legendary Lost Coast of Humboldt County, 3,000 ft. above the cloud line. This is where he learned the art of organic, sustainable farming and responsible agricultural practices. Over the next few years, he grew his network of like-minded individuals who wanted integrity in their growing processes, both here in the US and across the pond as well. Today, Mr. Ferla's state-of-the-art cannabis cultivation facilities meet the highest of standards, and I can personally attest to the love he has for his compost and the seriousness of its role in growing clean, healthy cannabis.

Now, according to Josh, "Genotypes are the DNA of a particular cannabis plant. Its genetic gene pool, if you will. Now, there will be different physical traits, phenotypes (fee-no-type), that show up after planting once it has been exposed to the environment (temps, humidity, indoor or outdoor stressors).

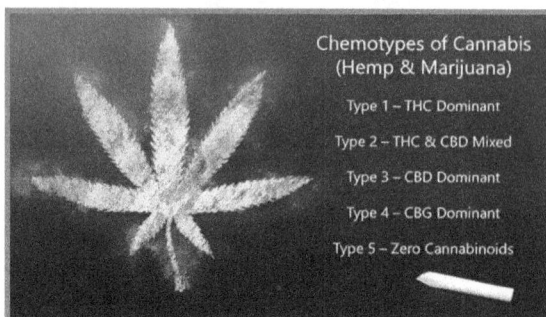

Chemotypes of Cannabis
(Hemp & Marijuana)

Type 1 – THC Dominant

Type 2 – THC & CBD Mixed

Type 3 – CBD Dominant

Type 4 – CBG Dominant

Type 5 – Zero Cannabinoids

These physical traits can range from the very subtle to the not-so-subtle differences in plant structure, color, growth pattern, or vigor. Kind of like you and your maternal siblings can look similar but different from each other, even though you share the same genotype—or genetic pool of material—and have been exposed to the same environment. Some of us tan better or burn easier than our siblings. Chemotypes, by definition, "... are often defined by the most abundant chemical profile produced by that individual and the concept has been useful in work done by chemical ecologists and natural product chemists."[19]

Josh explains even further with, "A chemotype is to plants as blue eyes, red hair, or inherited traits and health issues are to humans." Chemotypes characterize the most abundant chemical makeup, but also contain any potential deficiencies of the genetic material. So, even under perfect environmental conditions, you might get different physical attributes even though they come from the same gene pool. You see this in humans too; some families have twins and other strong resemblances to their children, other times kids with red hair are born to parents who have none. These are the expressions of the most abundant chemical makeup inherited from the genotype in that particular individual from the available gene pool, even including recessive genes.

> "For instance, the Purple Punch cannabis strain also contains a fair amount of anthocyanins (water soluble pigments that can appear red, purple, or blue in cannabis flowers). However, some of the plant's physical traits expressed under certain environmental conditions (phenotypes), and their chemical makeup (chemotypes), did not acquire a large enough amount of anthocyanin chemicals from the gene pool (genotype) to produce these vibrant colors. This occurs even under the perfect environmental conditions, when other chemotypes might otherwise express these colors from the same exact genotype or genetic material."

Now I have done my due diligence (thanks to Mr. Ferla). But if this is an area that gets your wheels turning and your questions burning, I urge you to look further into it. Plant science can be pretty cool.[20]

TERPENES

"Terps, terps, everywhere; in the stain on the wooden stair, in the shampoo in your hair,

In the magic of your bong, in the trichomes, thick and strong

Smell them here and taste them there; terps, terps, are everywhere ..."[21]

Terpenes are defined as "... the largest and most diverse group of naturally occurring compounds that are mostly found in plants, but larger classes of terpenes such as sterols and squalene can be found in animals. They are responsible for the fragrance, taste, and pigment of plants ... The common plant sources of terpenes are tea, thyme, cannabis, Spanish sage, and citrus fruits (e.g., lemon, orange, mandarin)."[22]

The more that I read about terpenes, the more impressed I am. Example, some plants can deploy an "indirect defense" where it actually puts out the call to the enemy of its enemies. For example, when white birch trees are under siege by moth caterpillars, the tree releases a blend of the terpenes ocimene and linalool. This terp blend attracts several species of birds that attack and feed on the caterpillars.[23] Nature is so smart!

So, what can terpenes do for humans? The saying goes, "your nose knows." If your snout finds a certain aroma welcoming or is disgusted by a scent, the theory is that it can be a clue to what your body may actually need. Research has shown this to be particularly helpful in mood or anxiety disorders.[24]

Let's take a look at the most popular terpenes that can be found in cannabis.

BETA CARYOPHYLLENE (BETA-CARRY-O-FILE-LEAN)

Is beta caryophyllene—or BCP for short—a cannabinoid? Or is it a terpene? It actually is both! BCP is often categorized as a cannabinoid, not a terpene, because it binds to CB2 cannabinoid receptors.

FLAVOR / AROMA
- CLOVE
- SPICY
- DRY
- WOODY

HEALTH EFFECT
- ANTIMICROBIAL
- ANTI-INFLAMMATORY
- NEUROPROTECTIVE

VAPORIZE AT
- 130°C
- 266°K

That being said, it also has the ability to dampen the effects of THC when taken together. BCP is also found in abundance in several legal herbs and spices such as cinnamon, basil, pepper, coriander, chestnut, sage, lavender, oregano, and rosemary, among others. It is even an FDA-approved food additive, and for this reason, some sources label BCP the "first dietary cannabinoid."[25]

Studies are showing that BCP could potentially curb addiction withdrawals, assist with wound healing, and even be applied as a tumor suppressant.[26]

DELTA-3-CARENE (CAR-EEN)

Delta-3-carene can smell like a sweet mix of pine, citrus, and wood, and can be found in pine and cedar trees, as well as rosemary. It is used as an insect repellent and in the cosmetic industry for perfumes.

FLAVOR / AROMA

- PINE
- CYPRESS
- ROSEMARY

HEALTH EFFECT

- ANTI-INFLAMMATORY
- BONE STIMULANT

VAPORIZE AT

- 171°C
- 340°K

Research is showing that this terpene can help with repairing damaged bones and fending off inflammation. Delta-3-carene is unique due to its ability to draw out liquids. This makes it a good candidate to be used as an antihistamine, or for any other issue that may need fluids whisked away. But alas, this is a double-edged sword, as this little guy is most likely the culprit for the dry eyes and cottonmouth that cannabis smokers combat.[27]

HUMULENE (HUM-A-LEEN)

What do beer and cannabis have in common? Hops! To be more specific, the terpene humulene, which smells of herbal spice and that classic peppery, hoppy bite. It can also be naturally found in cloves, sage, ginger, black pepper, and spearmint.

Humulene has strong anti-inflammatory properties and is still used today in Chinese medicine as an appetite suppressant.[28]

FLAVOR / AROMA

- BITTER
- PEPPERY
- FLORAL
- WOODY

HEALTH EFFECT

- ANTIBACTERIAL
- ANTI-INFLAMMATORY

VAPORIZE AT

- 106°C
- 222°K

LIMONENE (LEM-IN-NEEN)

FLAVOR / AROMA

- CITRUSY
- SWEET

HEALTH EFFECT

- ANTIBACTERIAL
- MOOD ELEVATION
- STRESS RELIEF

VAPORIZE AT

- 176°C
- 349°K

Limonene is one of the most common terpenes out there. You can find this lemony scent in everything from your body lotion to your cleaning supplies. It can also be used as a "green" solvent in itself. So please keep this in mind if you are into concentrates with "terp sauce," and are considering cranking up the heat on your rig.

On the medical side of things, limonene has been studied for its anti-inflammatory, anticancer, antiviral, and gut-protecting effects. When consumed via cannabis, the effects can be uplifting and used as a mood stabilizer.[29] It is also showing promise because "d-Limonene has also been used as a sorption promoter or accelerant for improving transdermal drug delivery and works by penetrating the skin to reversibly decrease barrier resistance." So, if the next cannabis topical you buy has limonene in the ingredients, you just might be getting more bang for your buck.[30]

LINALOOL (LIN-A-LOOOOL)

FLAVOR / AROMA

- FLORAL
- WOODY
- ROSE

HEALTH EFFECT

- ANTI-ANXIETY
- SEDATIVE

VAPORIZE AT

- 199°C
- 390°K

Would you agree that lavender is soothing and/or calming? What is giving off those effects is my favorite terpene, linalool, which can also be found in lavender, sage, rosemary, lemon balm, and bergamot.

This popular floral scent has been researched for uses as a natural aid for sleep issues, and as a calming agent for anxiety without the side effects of sedation, dependance, tolerance, or withdrawal symptoms.[31]

MYRCENE (MER-SEEN)

Myrcene is one of the most abundant, attractive-smelling terpenes found in cannabis. It can also be found in the oils of plants like hops, lemongrass, and citrus fruits.

In addition to the enticing smell of myrcene, it may aid other cannabinoids and terpenes in busting through the blood-brain barrier for better bioavailability. Cannabis strains that have over 0.5% myrcene are more likely to deliver the "couch lock" effects, and therefore would be known to the general public as an "indica." In turn, those with less than 0.5% would be leaning toward the giddy-up "sativa" end of the spectrum.

FLAVOR / AROMA
- CITRUSY
- SWEET

HEALTH EFFECT
- ANTIBACTERIAL
- MOOD ELEVATION
- STRESS RELIEF

VAPORIZE AT
- 176°C
- 349°K

Current research reports that some of the biological activities include sedation, antidiabetic, antioxidant, anti-inflammatory, antibacterial, and possible anticancer effects.

According to the National Library of Medicine, there seems to be a disagreement on whether myrcene, as a food additive, is safe or is a tumor-causing carcinogen. "The uncertainty of the safety of myrcene stems from studies conducted by the National Toxicology Program, USA (NTP) which has shown an increased incidence of kidney and liver neoplasms in rodents. In 2018, the FDA took regulatory action to no longer permit the use of β-myrcene as a food additive based on legal action taken against the FDA under the Delaney Clause (a federal health statute which prohibits FDA approval of any food additive which caused cancer in humans or animals). Importantly, the FDA confirmed that there was no safety concern for β-myrcene to public health under the conditions of its intended use.

Several other regulatory and scientific expert bodies have since argued that β-myrcene is safe under conditions of intended use as a flavoring substance and it must be noted that countless permitted food products continue to naturally contain significant levels of β-myrcene."[32]

So again, dabbers, you may want to back off the hellfire heat when inhaling terpenes in high concentrations. There is still so much that we don't know, and it is better to proceed with caution.

ALPHA & BETA PINENE (PINE-EEN)

α-PINENE	β-PINENE
FLAVOR / AROMA	**FLAVOR / AROMA**
• COOL　• PINEY • FRESH　• TURPENTINE • HERBAL	• GREEN HAY　• SPICY • PINEY　• WOODY
HEALTH EFFECT	**HEALTH EFFECT**
• ALERTNESS • MEMORY RETENTION	• ANTI-INFLAMMATORY • BRONCHODILATOR
VAPORIZE AT	**VAPORIZE AT**
• 156°C　• 312°K	• 165°C　• 329°K

Pinene is nature's king of the terpenes, and they can also be found in basil, dill, orange peels and yep, you guessed it—pine needles. There are two, the alpha and the beta, and they both come with their own unique attributes.

Research is looking into this rock star for its anti-inflammatory and anti-anxiety potential, plus its influence as a bronchodilator. Yes, the inhalation of this terpene will actually help open up your lungs! Studies have also reported that they may have the potential to reduce the number of lung cancer nodules, prevent gastric lesions, and show anticancer and antimicrobial promise.[33, 34]

FLAVONOIDS

Even though terpenes are getting all the attention these days, we cannot forget the mighty flavonoid!

CANNABIS FLAVONOIDS
how can flavonoids benefit you?

1 APIGENIN
- Anticancer
- Cardiovascular
- Anti-inflammatory

2 ANTHOCYANINS
- Antioxidant
- Anti-aging
- Antibacterial

3 BETA-SITOSTEROL
- Anti-atheroginic
- Anti-inflammatory
- Anti-carcinogenic

4 CANNFLAVIN A
- Anti-aggresive
- Anti-inflammatory
- Neuroprotective

5 CANNFLAVIN B
- Antioxidant
- Anticancer
- Pain killing

6 ISOVITEXIN
- Antioxidant
- Anticancer
- Anti-inflammatory

7 VITEXIN
- Anticancer
- Anti-hyperalgesic
- Neuroprotective

8 SILYMARIN
- Antioxidant
- Cardioprotective
- Anti-inflammatory

9 QUERCETIN
- Antioxidant
- Cardiovascular
- Anti-obesity

10 ORIENTIN
- Antiviral
- Vasodilatation
- Cardioprotective

11 LUTEOLIN
- Anticancer
- Neuroprotective
- Immunomodulatory

12 KAEMPFEROL
- Antimicrobial
- Antioxidant
- Antitumor

The National Library of Medicine reports that "Currently there are about 6000 flavonoids that contribute to the colourful pigments of fruits, herbs, vegetables and medicinal plants."

So, flavonoids have nothing to do with flavor (thanks, science, for making it confusing), but are actually in charge of the color of plants. Those amazing fall colors that we all love so much are brought to us by the flavonoid anthocyanins. When the cooler air comes to town, the chlorophyll begins to break down and allows for these colors to shine through.

In fruits they attract pollinators and therefore help with seed and spore germination and the growth and development of said seedlings. Flavonoids also play a part in toughening up for frosts, freezing tolerance, and resistance to drought.

Why is this important to the cannabis consumer? Because flavonoids also have medicinal properties such as anti-inflammatory, anti-mutagenic, and anti-carcinogenic superpowers.[35]

PLANT ANATOMY

And where are all of these amazing plant attributes housed, you may ask? Why, they are stored in the totally tubular oddities you see in the picture on the left called trichomes (try-combs), also known as the "frost" located on the outside of the plant.

Per Chapter 4 of the amazingly named paper, "The Botanical Dance of Death: Programmed Cell Death in Plants" we learn that "Trichomes are shoot epidermal hairs, found on the majority of plants, and are composed of either single or several cells (Esau, 1977). They play various protective roles, such as being a mechanical barrier to insect herbivores, filtering UV light and reducing respiration (Fordyce and Agrawal, 2001; Karabourniotis et al., 1992; Levin, 1973; Ripley et al., 1999; Van Dam and Hare, 1998)."[36]

So, one reason the sticky icky is sticky is to deter some pests from invading and setting up shop.

LANDRACES

A landrace strain is a pure cannabis plant that is exactly how and where God put it. This term is used to indicate the purity of its genetics, therefore meaning it has never been sliced, diced, or bastardized. "Sativa" landraces are originally from hot climates such as Africa, Jamaica, and South America. "Indica" landraces, on the other hand, are from cooler climates like the Afghan Mountains. A few famous landrace strains are Lambs Bread, Hindu Kush, Durban Poison, and Panama Red.

We have heard many growers throw around the term "landrace" when marketing their offerings. But are there truly any real landrace strains left in this labradoodle world? Some say yes and some say no. Just about everything on the dispensary shelves is a hybrid of some sort. So, there are those that spend their days "hunting" the four corners of our planet for the genotypes and phenotypes of moons gone by to build cannabis genetic bases in hopes of creating a baseline. Enter David Watson stage left …

In the world of marijuana maestros, the co-founder of HortaPharm, David Watson, was a deity among men. He had collected the world's most extensive library of cannabis seeds known to man.[37]

As someone who was a lifetime member of the Seed Savers Exchange in the United States, it's safe to say that the guy really dug his seeds. And the potential for different medical applications, depending on the genetics, turned David's attention toward collecting cannabis seeds. In his travels during this quest, he had noticed that the worldwide attempts to wipe this plant out were putting more than a dent into the upper crust of the plant's genetic gene pool. So, with all possible speed Mr. Watson traveled to the far corners of the earth collecting what he could.

In 1994 he applied to the Dutch Ministry of Health for a license to grow cannabis, and in 1997 he and his business partner, Robert Clarke, became the first legal cannabis grow operation for pharmaceutical research.

When interviewed by Bill Breen in 2004, he was asked what exactly he was looking for in a cannabis plant. David had said, "I want varieties that have unusual characteristics in their growth or flowering period, or new and unusual sources of cannabinoids." And when he was asked why, he replied in a true salt of the earth fashion with, "We were really interested in bringing cannabis back into mainstream medicine."[38]

The partners began HortaPharm, and with a proprietary process they became the planet's first breeder to develop homozygote cannabis called "selfing." This technique, in which both sets of chromosomes are identical, allows for the mass production of the cannabis plant with the same cannabinoid profile every time.

This is huge! Because this is exactly what is needed if we are to turn botanicals into standard medications. It is with sadness that I report that our industry lost this pioneer in the first month of 2025. Mr. Watson made our world a better place and now I hope he is resting peacefully.

INDICA, SATIVA AND HYBRIDS

We have all heard these terms before. Indica is supposed to give sedative effects of being "in-da-couch." Sativas are labeled as giving the opposite effects, offering the giddy-up that some of us lack. And then there is the hybrid, which claims to be a mix of both. To say that a flower "leans" one way or the other is again said to dictate if the product will be more sedative or energizing.

Sorry guys, but these terms are frankly misleading. Sativa and indica can be used when describing the physical attributes of how the plant grows and looks to the naked eye. But these terms have little to do with what is actually in the plant, chemically speaking.

I have spoken to many inquirers on the subject, and they are amazed when I tell them that THC was only a portion of the story when it came to their beloved "sativas." I explained that it was the terpenes, such as pinene or limonene, that gave them the uplifting feeling they craved with their high.

While on the subject of what's in a name, I'm going to push you a bit further. Do not put too much stock into a strain's name. You could take three separate grams of Purple Punch, from three different locations, and the odds are that they would all have different profiles. By profiles, I mean the concentration of different cannabinoid and terpene amounts from the test results. Hell, I've named strains before myself. I was presented with a cross of Granddaddy Purple and a Durban Poison and asked what it was called for proper entry into the system. The response I got was a shoulder shrug and "what should we call it?" So, I deemed it Granddaddy Durban, and so it was.

1:1 RATIOS

Now I have only run across a few people that have very high tolerances for THC, but when they combine it with CBD, it puts them in a completely different frame of mind. One fella I know has smoked heavy amounts of marijuana on every single continent, yet when we shared a bowl of Cannatonic #4 (high CBD) with Apollo 13 bubble hash (high THC) sprinkled on top, he was floored! The vast majority of us will not feel this type of effect, but this is a good example of how different mixtures of cannabinoids can have different effects on each of us.

Most of us don't usually consider mixing the two cannabinoids, unless you are like me that adores a natural 1:1 ratio for pain relief without much of a high. By "natural," I mean both THC and CBD are a part of the plant's genetics and have close to even amounts of each cannabinoid. There are plenty of products out there that are sold as a 1:1, but most of them are just stripped-down THC distillate mixed with CBD isolate. This splicing and dicing of the cannabis plant gives different results than when you keep as much of the plant together as possible.

Unfortunately, you'll be hard-pressed to find true 1:1 flower in retail shops. When I approach growers about this their answers are all the same. "It doesn't sell." Or "It doesn't yield enough to make it worth my time." Ugh. I believe that if retailers and patients alike were educated on the benefits of this ratio, the shops would sell it in abundance. But instead, we are stuck with mixing THC strains with hemp flower for the CBD.

SOME WELL-KNOWN 1:1 STRAINS INCLUDE:

1. HARLEQUIN
2. STARTONIC
3. GIRL POWER
4. AC/DC
5. PENNYWISE
6. MILK & COOKIES

I am going to jump ahead here briefly to help make sure that the following section makes a little more sense. Before we get into the different ways someone can use cannabis, I want you to understand that the amount of product that gets into your system depends not on just the volume you take, but on how you take it. This is known as bioavailability, and is defined as, "When a substance such as a medicine or supplement enters your system, the portion of the total substance introduces which can effectively create a response determines that substance's bioavailability. The bioavailability of a substance can fluctuate, depending on the route of administration.

"Intravenous administration, or a direct line into the bloodstream, is typically considered 100% bioavailability, as all of the substance will reach target cells. In oral administration routes, AKA when you take a pill, the amount of medicine or supplement you receive depends on many factors, including your diet and your personal metabolism."[39]

That being said, how much and how fast you are affected has almost everything to do with how you choose to take your cannabis. Notice that I said "almost"? That is because genetics and tolerance will also have their say in how and when your weed kicks in as well.

And then there is the decarboxylation (dee-car-box-a-lay-shun) we were talking about when changing acid forms (THCA + heat = THC). Cannabinoids all have different boiling points, and unless you want to scorch your stash to ash, you should know how hot is too hot.

THCA	CBN
220-240°F	365°F
CBDA	CBGA
200-220°F	200-220°F
CBCA	THCV
283°F	428°F

Ex: You want to make cannabis cookies with some shake you bought at your local pot shop. You know you have to change the THCA to THC by decarbing the plant matter first, but if you pop it in the oven at 400 degrees you will be cooking off all of the THC that was intended for your tagalongs.[40]

THE FIVE METHODS OF INTAKE

Now we can get into the top five most common ways to partake. These are inhaling, ingesting, sublingually, topical application, and bringing up the rear—rectally.

INHALING: JOINTS VS. VAPORIZING VS. CARTRIDGES

The quickest route, outside of sticking a needle in your arm (nobody should ever, ever do this), is to inhale. You can roll a joint or a blunt. You can pack a bowl, fire up a bong, or use a dry herb vaporizer. The dried flower of the cannabis plant (buds, nugs or the thousand other names to call it) is still the most popular method of consumption.[41]

Once you roll it up and set a flame to it, you are now not only inhaling the herb, but also the paper and the carcinogens common with the whole smoking process. When you use a bong or bowl (I recommend glass), you are getting the herb and the carcinogens. But if you choose to use a dry herb vaporizer you are getting nothing but the plant with each hit. This is due to the process of vaporization, where you are applying heat to the herb without actually burning the plant matter. After finishing what you put into the vape, you will not find ashes, as you would in a bowl or bong. What you will find is what looks like crispy, dry tobacco.

Studies have shown that the consumer can get up to 80% of the cannabinoids and terpenes (the good stuff) when vaporized, compared to the old school method where you are only getting up to 30% of the original goodness.[42]

I know, I know. Most of us old schoolers still prefer classic combustion to healthier alternatives. Maybe it's the draw into the lungs, maybe it's the release on exhale, or maybe the ceremonial preparation of rolling a joint or stuffing your favorite bong. Regardless of our personal reasons, at least we have choices these days when it comes to how we smoke our cannabis.

> Tip: I know you're not supposed to ask how the sausage is made, but you should know what's in your pre-rolls. Is it trim, buds or a mix of both? I'd say it's safe to say that any freebee added on is going to be useless trim that the processor is just trying to make a buck on. But it only takes one dusty pre-roll to lose a customer forever, so when one is being bought by choice always offer the bud.

Things have become a bit more convenient for those who choose to inhale their marijuana with the invention of the cartridge. They are small, generally don't have a smell to them, and they seem to last forever. But hear me and heed me when I say that it is not the same as smoking flower. Not even a little bit.

For starters, it isn't a flower. It is an end result of an extraction of the cannabis plant. It can be made from trim leaves or from the buds or from both. It is then processed by using solvents (we'll get into the different types later), and the end product is the highly concentrated oil product you see in your cartridges. Straight distillate carts are generally a very pale gold color, unless they are exposed to too much sunlight, in which case they will start to turn a darker color as the oil oxidizes. Resin and rosin carts, on the other hand, start out much darker, as there is more plant matter left behind in the end product.

Vaping and vaporizing use two completely different products. As mentioned above, vaporizing is using the dried flower, while vaping is using concentrated cannabis. Vaping, whether it's cannabis or nicotine, has been a very real health concern for years. The illicit market, in true drug dealer fashion, has been making black market carts that have been repeatedly "stepped on," meaning that they take the original product and keep cutting the oil with Lord knows what to stretch their base product.

But there is a way for you to check to see if it's been severely diluted. Simply find the bubble in the oil and then flip your cart upside down. If the bubble races to the other end, it has been diluted. With uncut concentrates, the bubble will not move, or if it does, it will be extremely slow about it. This of course is not foolproof, just a little trick I picked up along the way.

Carts can come in a cylinder shape or in a pod shape. One is not better than the other, although they each use different batteries. It just comes down to a matter of preference.

Carts are notorious for malfunctioning. They can leak all over, clog up from the oil getting into the mouthpiece (yuck), or even melt if the battery temps are too hot. I have had more than one vaper come across my path whining that they clogged their tank or wasted a ton of expensive product just trying to get it in the damn thing. You can pick up any stick or pod battery from a smoke shop for cheap; try to get one with a temperature dial, and it'll be well worth it.

CONCENTRATES

Ahh, the sweating, coughing, punch in the face of THC that entices those who are looking for the stronger effects of cannabis. I can see why some people can be concerned about the potency of some of today's cannabis products. Concentrates need to be respected, with cannabinoid percentages creeping in at over 90%.

Even though they are not my personal preference, I do believe that these concentrates, and their potency levels, do have their place in the world for cannabis medical patients. When a person is battling off-the-charts pain from chemo, or is trying to kick an opioid addiction, sometimes the only thing that will touch the pain is the one-two punch of concentrates. And when given proper direction, the patient can begin to wean themselves down to lower THC percentages over time, and therefore in theory will need less medication for their conditions.

There are several different ways to extract all of the goodies that a cannabis plant has to offer. Different methods will not only have an effect on the potency of the end product but can also have varying consistencies. My hope for you is that you'll be able to spot the extraction method based upon what it looks like on the shelf, and then not only be able to make confident guesses as to the general ballpark of the potency, but also how much of the original plant is still intact.

In the following section you will see the terms "plant matter" and "total cannabinoids" used quite a bit. Plant matter refers to the entire plant. Not only cannabinoids, terpenes, and flavonoids, but chlorophyll, lipids, waxes, and other compounds in the natural state of the plant. Total cannabinoids refer to the complete count of not only THC and CBD percentages, but also any cannabinoids detected that show up in testing, regardless of their low numbers.

Since concentrate knowledge is one part plant science and one part chemistry (neither one my strong suit), I have asked someone who knows these two subjects intimately to review and comment in the following section for accuracy and clarity.

Raven Ariola, M.S. began his official cannabis career providing hands-on technical analysis and solutions to nearly every licensed cultivation and processing facility in Pennsylvania. It was in these medical cannabis testing labs, licensed grow facilities, and vertically integrated dispensaries that Raven saw the true results of what strong education can do for our rapidly growing industry.

He has received his degree in Medical Cannabis Sciences & Therapeutics from the University of Maryland School of Pharmacy, which is the nation's first graduate program studying cannabis science. He then served as the Director of Education for the Medical Cannabis Student Association. He is also responsible for the wildly popular podcast Plants Saved My Life, which offers the very personal experiences (mine included) that people have had with using plants as medicine.

DIFFERENT EXTRACTION METHODS

SOLVENTS VS. SOLVENTLESS

Many solvents can be used when extracting cannabis for concentrates, but they can also be done without them. Using chemicals to pull out the desired plant compounds leads to some of the solvent being left behind. The product then needs to be run through a "purge" to clean up the product as much as possible. Most states have a list of "acceptable" levels of chemicals allowed in the end product, which can range from alcohols to gasses such as butane. Testing for these leftovers is crucial, especially for those who use concentrates as medicine. The very last thing a sick person needs is to intake these residuals at potentially toxic levels.

STRAIN

WOODY OG

Even though some processors believe that concentrating the plant will "clean up" any contaminants, they are mistaken. In their attempts to concentrate the terpenes and cannabinoids, they are also concentrating any pesticides, heavy metals, and impurities as well.

But the purge is an unnecessary step when you don't use solvents to begin with. Pressure and heat can be used and will give you rosin in the end. Or you can use mesh bags to either add ice water, or without anything at all, to produce hash.

Some will argue that ice and water are not to be considered "solventless," as you are in fact using something to pull the goodies off of the plant. Others will go another way and say the CO_2 must be included as "solventless" because it is a natural product (even if it is converted from a gas to a liquid), like water and ice. It all comes down to who you ask.

It is these varying opinions that make the need for standardization crucial. When asking Raven this question, his educated opinion was, "I'd define solventless as using NO solvent, including CO_2. Although water is the universal solvent, it maintains the integrity of cannabinoids and terpenes. Anything using only heat and/or water is considered to be solventless."

HASHISH

Hash is old, old school. In fact, it has been around for hundreds of years, and originated in places such as Morocco, Afghanistan, Nepal, Iran, and Lebanon.[43]

This concentrate is made by collecting and pressing the trichomes into a thick, tarry substance. It is then pressed into blocks or turned into oil. It is most commonly smoked or added to foods and teas.[44]

When speaking of hashish, one must give glory to Frenchy Cannoli. It has been said that he treated creating hash like raising a fine wine. He was relentless in his pursuit of obtaining and then aging this eras-old concentrate. I can think of no other person who respected this ancient way of concentrating cannabis more, and he was tireless in his teachings to spread the methods of yesteryears. If you are interested in the true art of hash making, I urge you to look into the education Frenchy has left behind for us.[45]

ICE WATER/BUBBLE HASH

Modern hash is processed differently and is actually really hard to find in the retail shops. If I had to guess it would be because any leftover plant matter is being turned into higher THC percentage (and higher dollar worth) distillate, plus it is a total pain in the ass to make. The process is very hands-on and is more labor-intensive than most processors are willing to do. Even though solventless is the most cost-efficient way to get started in extractions, the yield of only 5%-15% of weight is less than ideal for processors.

Bubble hash was given its name due to the product actually bubbling when set on fire. It's made by using a series of mesh bags with varying sized holes and simple ice water. The shimmying and shaking of the mesh bags will separate the partially frozen trichomes from the rest of the plant matter. One will also need a freeze dryer to rid the concentrate of excess moisture. The end product, once dry, will look crumbly and dark brown. This can be used as is, or further pressed into rosin.

This can also be done without the ice water, known as "dry sift," which is pretty much just kief, as the process is just knocking off the cannabinoid and terpene-filled trichomes.

Consumers have reported that by going this route the end product has less "flavor," which is probably due to beating up the trichomes during the extraction process. You can expect the potency to range from 55% to 65% total cannabinoids.

PRESSURE AND HEAT

The simple actions of applying the right temperature and then pressing the living hell out of a bud will give you a solventless concentrate called rosin.

This is sometimes referred to as "squishing," and the end result is a dark and thick syrupy product. The color not only comes from the whole plant properties, but also from burnt plant matter, which makes rosin a partial decarbed product.

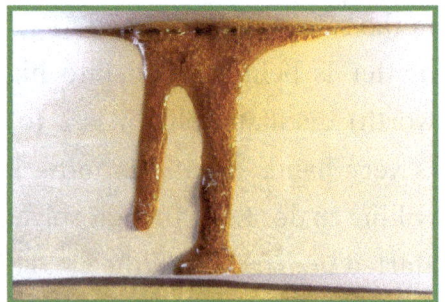

Just about anyone who is into concentrates has tried to produce rosin by putting a bud between two pieces of wax paper and using a hair straightener in an attempt to squeeze out the concentrate. As these folks have learned at the expense of a wasted nug or two—the process doesn't require a change to the method, but needs to be done on a much, much bigger scale with a much bigger hair straightener.

As with any high-heat extraction, the lesser terpenes and cannabinoids will be cooked off in the process, and therefore the potency numbers will be lower than some other methods. You can expect the end product strength to come in between 60% and 80% total cannabinoids (depending on what you're working with). And if you are interested in the yields, it's typically about 10% of however much flower is used, according to Raven.

CO_2 (CARBON DIOXIDE)

Carbon dioxide, according to Britannica, is well known for its use as a refrigerant, in fire extinguishers, coal blasting, and promoting the growth of plants in green houses, among other things.[46] Now we can add cannabis extraction to this list. Making concentrates using CO_2 is done by

turning this natural gas into a liquid and then applying it as a solvent.

This method isn't as harsh on the plant and therefore leaves more of the original plant intact. But you will lose some of the minor terpenes, as they are usually the first to go in using the majority of extraction methods. When using CO_2, you can have a more stable shelf life, and the product can last up to a year with minimal degradation if refrigerated to preserve the cannabinoids and terpenes. This is also assuming the concentrate is only exposed to minimal light and oxygen.[47]

The end product consistency is a lot like molasses in color and texture, and the potency can range from 60% to 80% total cannabinoids.[48]

BHO (BUTANE HASH OIL)

Using butane was once the most popular extraction method in retail, although I believe that distillate may be giving it a run for its money these days. In hearing of homemade extractions, and the garages they have leveled over the years, you can almost guarantee that it was due to the reckless use of butane and their attempts to purge.

After the butane, propane, or other "anes" (hydrocarbons) have been run through the plant matter, "you are then left with roughly 95% cannabis oil and 5% propane or butane residual solvents in your collection pot. At this point it still needs the 72-hour purge."[49]

Different times and temps used during the purge will give you the different consistencies that you see in the shops. Some are shatter (glass-like), some are waxy and look like honeycombs, while others will look like applesauce or whipped butter (badder, in retail speak). These physical consistencies play a role in what concentrate you may choose. Some prefer to "work with" badder for easy scooping, instead of shatter that breaks like glass and can fly everywhere. Butane extractions will still need to be decarbed by heat to turn the THCA into THC, and these can test out anywhere from 80% to 90% total cannabinoids.

Before the days of solvent restrictions, homogeneity, and "acceptable limits," extractionists were just learning the art of the purge. A lot of outbuildings burned down, and a lot of people consumed some pretty nasty concentrates, or "butane soup" as it is also known.

Yes, these guys also had to submit test results and were often turned away with their pizza boxes filled with slabs of shatter with the warning to "do better," before trying to get in the door again. But these were the days when a fully stocked display case with questionable offerings was better than having only a handful of pricey stellar products. Concentrates are generally only purchased by the younger generation and therefore the bang for your buck is definitely top priority. Shady or ignorant, those were the times.

You could physically see who was buying the cheap "butane soup." Their skin was gray, eyes yellowed, and they were always cranky. Attempts to sway them toward cleaner concentrates were always met with an argument over pricing, and then the purchase of the same old crap.

DISTILLATION

You can thank distillate for getting rid of the weedy taste in your edibles. Distillate was a game changer when it made its first appearance in the cannabis market. It pushed cartridges into the daylight, it was an easier, more consistent product to infuse edibles with, and is generally free of everything except the desired THC.

Think along the lines of a gin mill south of the Mason-Dixon Line. Everything is broken down to the compound level, then temperature is used to cook off everything but the THC (sometimes CBD). More often than not, cannabis processors will take the plant and turn it into a butane extraction before using the distillate process to refine it even further. Distillate is considered to be a single, completely decarbed compound product—unless terpenes are reintroduced—and can test out in the mid to high 90% range.

Tip: If your distillate is being difficult in that you cannot seem to get it out of the syringe, you can either rub it between your hands or run it under warm water to get it to loosen up. When doing the latter, make sure you don't do it for too long. If the product gets too viscous, it will all come dripping out once you have removed the cap.

THCA DIAMONDS AND SAUCE

These "diamonds," sometimes called "sand," are just about as close as you can get to pure THCA (96%–99.9%), although you may find very small amounts of other cannabinoids and terpenes in the end product (1%–4%). THCA diamonds are considered the most potent single cannabinoid extract option currently available.

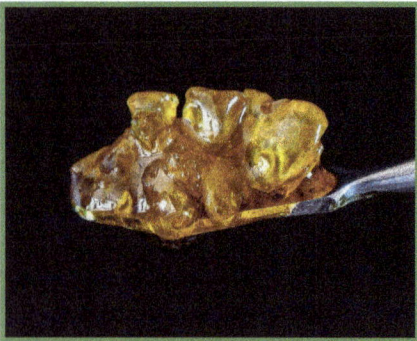

So how can you tell how potent your diamonds will be just by looking at them? The diamonds highest in THC will be a stark snow white. If there are some terpenes and/or cannabinoids that hang around, the product will have an amber or yellowish hue.[50] These "leftovers" are not a bad thing. If I was shopping for diamonds, I would actually choose the less pristine option for the added terpenes and cannabinoids.

But the visual purity of the diamonds will be lost when combined with "sauce," which is liquified terpenes mixed in for flavor and potential effects. Also, please remember my warning about inhaling terpenes in high concentrations with high heat once you get your purchase home.

Now I will leave the explanation of how these diamonds are made to Raven: "The process itself is actually pretty neat-technicians start with a processed extract, then the crystals are "grown" in mason jars using time and agitation when necessary. Remember the old science fairs where you'd scratch a glass, and salt would form? Same concept in crystal formation of THCA diamonds."

ALCOHOL

According to Johnsons Environmental Products, "Food grade alcohol" means ethyl alcohol that is safe for human consumption because of its purity (i.e., lack of additives). Period. Food grade alcohol goes by many names in the industry, including food grade ethanol, nondenatured alcohol, grain alcohol, 190 proof grain, food grade EtOH, and anhydrous ethanol.[51]

As in any commercial production, people are always trying to cut corners to save a buck. Many cannabis processors will reach for the cheaper (and unacceptable) "denatured alcohol," which brings nasty carcinogens into the mix.

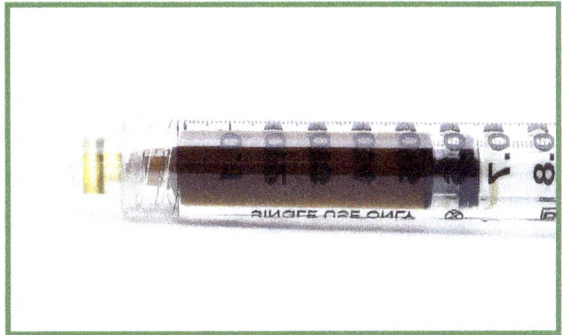

Now just because most of the above are considered "safe," does not mean that the extraction doesn't need to be purged. There is still a boatload of unwanted solvent after this extraction process, all of which must be flushed to meet any state sanctioned acceptable levels.

This method will give you the darkest color of all of the different extractions, as it holds onto the most plant matter, and will give you a whole plant extract that will generally test out between 50% and 75% total cannabinoids.

It is also the process most widely used for Rick Simpson Oil (RSO) or fully extracted cannabis oil (FECO). If you want to get technical, RSO is/ was extracted with naphtha. "Humans commonly use petroleum naphtha as a solvent. It can be found in various cleaning agents where its low evaporation point comes in handy, and works as a dilution agent for paints, varnish, and asphalt. Dry-cleaning businesses also use naphtha in their operations."[52] Hence the reason for getting away from this solvent.

The "proposed" regimen for taking this extraction for the purposes of combating chemotherapy and cancer, is to take 90 grams in 60 days. This is a huge ask, especially for those brand-spanking-new to cannabis. Even with the beginning doses starting at a half of the size of a grain of rice, the struggle is real. Most will get a tolerance to this tarry substance rather quickly but believe me when I tell you that the first two weeks will be a challenge.

I do have to mention that the RSO acronym is another frustrating bit of vernacular to some of us because it references the name of a "who" rather than "what" the product actually is. FECO is the correct way to reference this type of product. I know. There are more than a few desired changes to the language used in this industry, but I promise it's only for a better understanding of the marijuana in our lives.

"LIVE" VS. "CURED" CONCENTRATES

"Live" is when the plant is pulled out of the ground and is directly frozen at some pretty wicked cold temps to flash freeze all of the trichomes prior to extraction.

This method will give you more of the original plant attributes and its flavors. "Cured" means that the plant was pulled and then dried before the extraction. And it should be taken into consideration that a cannabis plant can lose up to 75% of terpenes during the harvesting, drying, and curing process. This is also why you'll see "live" concentrates costing more in shops than the "cured" variety.

Two common questions often asked about concentrates are whether you can add them to your flower, and at what temperature you should smoke them at.

As anyone can tell just by looking at a dispensary menu, yes, you can in fact add concentrates to your flower, as infused joints are a big hit with consumers. But understand that adding any type of concentrate to your flower will increase the potency, and this should always be taken into consideration if you want to remain consistent with your dosages. It will also be a bit messier, as the resin will be thicker than if it was just flower alone.

Under this category you will find variations of "tarantula legs" and "moonrocks." The tarantula leg is a joint rolled in concentrate (usually hash oil unless specified otherwise) and then rolled again in kief or hash, giving it the appearance of a fuzzy spider leg.

Moonrocks are the same concept without the paper. A bud is rolled in concentrate and then rolled again in hash or kief. Either of these will take your THC percentage rates from the mid-20s to the mid-60s.

As for the ideal temperature when smoking cannabis concentrates out of a rig (basically a bong for concentrates), it again comes down to who you ask. Some choose a hellfire temp to make sure all of the THCA is decarbed into THC smoke, wasting nothing. For those of us who have common sense, it doesn't have to be explained why inhaling a product at 700+ degrees is bad for your lungs. The other opinion is that "you have to waste it to taste it." Lower temperatures will allow for some of the more robust terpenes and cannabinoids to survive the trip to your lungs, but you may be leaving some of the nondecarbed THCA behind.[53]

ACRONYMS TO KNOW

FECO	FULLY EXTRACTED CANNABIS OIL
RSO	RICK SIMPSON OIL
MCT	MEDIUM-CHAIN TRIGLYCERIDES (FROM COCONUT OR PALM KERNEL OIL)
HCFSE	HIGH CANNABINOID FULL SPECTRUM EXTRACT
HTFSE	HIGH TERPENE FULL SPECTRUM EXTRACT
BHO	BUTANE HASH OIL
MIP	MARIJUANA INFUSED PRODUCT
PPM	PARTS PER MILLION

EDIBLES

Most people are shocked when I tell them that when they eat an edible, at best they are actually only getting up to 30% of the THC they just ate. When your cookie or gummy goes straight down the hatch, it is run through the gauntlet of our digestive system and loses its punch as it is being absorbed along the way. To top it off, THC (Delta-9) is completely changed at the chemical compound level once it hits the liver.[54] Stay with me here folks.

We have a liver enzyme called P450, and according to the Mayo Clinic, "The human body uses cytochrome P450 enzymes to process medications. Because of inherited (genetic) traits that cause variations in these enzymes, medications may affect each person differently."[55]

This enzyme can actually make our medications more or less potent, depending on the drug. Our nonintoxicating friend CBD is well known for blocking the potency of drugs metabolized by this enzyme.[56]

P450 is the magician that changes the THC that we started with into 11-Hydroxy THC, and therefore alters the effects. Many people report that eating something infused with THC and smoking THC result in very different highs. I have to agree, because no matter how many chances I give

11-Hydroxy THC, we just don't get along.

Ingesting cannabis can take anywhere from 30 minutes to a full two hours to kick in. This is when people tend to lose their patience and add more edibles into the mix, thinking that it's not working. Rookie mistake. Your metabolism, whether you took them on a full stomach, and/or your tolerances have everything to do with your projected launch time.

We have all heard the term "low and slow" when it comes to taking edibles, and I stress this point again for those of you in the cheap seats.

These little nuggets of extraction covered in sugar can last for hours on end, and if you hit the boxing ring too hard, too fast, well ... down goes Frazier. What also happens is that you are not any closer to figuring out what your milligram "sweet spot" really is. In the long run, you'll end up spending way more money on finding the right dose and product line.

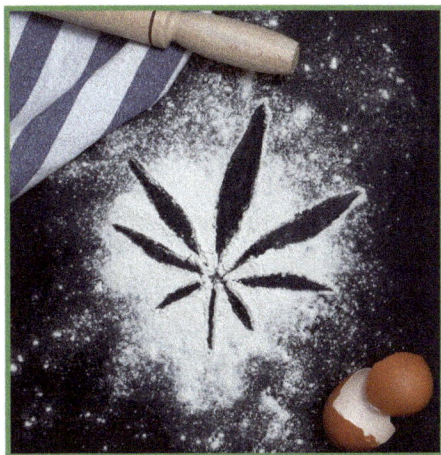

Someone who works behind a cannabis counter long enough will eventually get to know the regular customers. There was a young man who was attending classes at the university up the road, and like clockwork he would come in every Thursday after school for his treasured flower. One day Jack cheerfully bounced into the med room and asked for 25 Rice Krispy treats for a skiing trip he was taking with his fraternity brothers. The wise old elder in me rose up, and warnings of how edibles are different came spilling out of my mouth; the 50 mg treat would pack a punch in a way that he was not accustomed to.

He humored me with a nod and then a request for the total, so I began to bag up the treats. I wished him luck and sent him on his way to tackle the mountain.

The following week, he returned to the counter via crutches. "Wasn't wrong, was I Jack?" I scolded. Bashfully he told me the backstory of how they ate the edibles about an hour before getting on the chairlift and found that once up there they couldn't get down. They were so high that they just laid around at the lift drop off point for hours until they began to come down. Jack wasn't over his buzz as much as he thought he was before making the trip down the hill and misjudged the girth of a lone pine tree. He snapped his femur in two places and would need corrective surgery in the very near future. Still shaking my head at him, I sent him on his way with some flower to help with the pain.

SUBLINGUAL

There is also a second way to orally ingest your cannabis. The term sublingual comes from Latin, meaning "under the tongue," and is usually utilized using hard candies and tinctures.

Tinctures have become more and more popular over the years. Maybe it's because the name and the delivery method presents itself as more "medicinal," as opposed to the appearance of edibles being halfway between medicine and candy. I honestly can't even pretend to know how stigmas get attached to things. I'd like to think that we are evolving into a society that can see the potential medical benefits of going the sublingual route; however, I will not be holding my breath on this.

Tinctures, according to our dusty pharmacopeia, are actually alcohol based and not oil based, as you see in retail shops. These drops are meant to be placed under the tongue for optimal absorption in hopes that skipping the road trip through our digestive system, and the hard right turn toward liver conversion, will lead to more of the product making it into the bloodstream.

Research reports that consuming cannabis this way can result in the effects occurring in as little as 20 minutes, lasting from six to eight hours, and offering bioavailability of 40%–50% of your initial milligram intake.[57, 58]

We now know that just chomping down and swallowing an infused hard candy can take up to two hours to kick in, also resulting in the loss of all the original D9 THC due to the liver conversion into 11-Hydroxy THC. I usually recommend that people taking hard candy edibles should let it hang out in their mouth for a while. It can't hurt (dentists will disagree), and you may just get your desired effects quicker and with a bit more potency.

But what about those who have genetic differences when it comes to how their body processes drugs?

We have all heard the stories about someone that can eat hundreds of mgs of THC and not feel a thing. I had a co-worker who was one of these people. Hudson had pretty much given up on any other method of intake outside of smoking it, and he saw any additional attempts to gain relief from edibles as a waste of money. So, at a company Sunday barbeque I approached him with the idea of trying an edible but going the sublingual route this time. There was a novel, 25 mg Tic Tac-like product that was perfect for this kind of experiment. I gave him the lowdown on my theory that his liver enzyme was out of whack, and that it changes the way his body processes ingested THC. Hudson shrugged his shoulders and said, "I'm game."

Since it was my idea, I dug the tiny piece of candy out of my stash box and instructed him to let it melt in his mouth for as long as he could stand it. These were the days when processors weren't focused on taste, as they were still struggling with getting their cannabinoid numbers consistent. Therefore, most of the products tasted like bong water.

As a dog day of summer crept along, I had almost forgotten about our morning guinea pig session until I heard the telltale giggle that is unique to an infused edible. Peeking my head out of the kitchen, I saw Hudson shaking what his mama gave him and whistling along with the tune coming out of the speakers as he flipped burgers. "You're feeling it, aren't you?" I said with a curious grin.

"This is fantastic Ang. I've never felt weed like this before," he said with elation. Pleased with myself for a successful trial, I had him repeat the reason behind his newfound method of intake to ensure he had it right so he could pass the knowledge on to our patients.

TOPICALS VS. PATCHES

By mass, our skin is the human body's largest organ. Ointments, salves, and plant matter have been applied to the human skin since the beginning of time, but the transdermal application of cannabis didn't get any traction until technology caught up during the last third of the 20th century.[59]

Both topical and transdermal patches are applied to the skin, so what is the difference? Topicals target exactly what their name suggests. They are meant for the treatments of medical issues that are on the top of our skin, like rashes. On the other hand, transdermal patches are made to get the intended medicine into the bloodstream. This is a sure way to bypass the digestive tract and any liver conversions during a first pass metabolism, and therefore (in theory) will have greater bioavailability than taking cannabis orally.[60]

Topicals can be lotions, creams, oils, or anything that you rub into your skin. Generally, the effect can be felt in as little as a couple of minutes and can last as long as a couple of hours. The bioavailability isn't great at 5%–10% due to our mighty skin barrier, but topicals can be great for on-the-go inflammation and surface nerve and joint pain, as it is applied at the source.[61]

Of course, this is assuming the product does not reek like weed. The cannabis industry is still struggling with getting the pot smell out of topicals. We've come a long way, but still have further to go when it comes to attending to our skin with cannabis. The last thing you want to do is stink up the joint (pun intended) when you didn't even smoke anything!

I personally am a big supporter of topicals for their skincare benefits alone. Being from a state that is shaped like a mitten, you can imagine how unreasonable the winters are here. Over the years, with a ton of trial and error, I have found that CBD/CBC in a cream-based product does an amazing job at protecting my aging Polish skin.

Research is showing that not only are topicals great for pain caused by inflammation, but they can do some of the heavy lifting when it comes to more serious skin conditions such as wound healing, psoriasis, and melanoma. Granted, these topicals are usually super concentrated variations of FECO (RSO), but still show promise of being a nonintoxicating aid nonetheless.[62]

TRANSDERMAL PATCHES

Even though these patches are not really cost-efficient for everyday use, I'm still a groupie of the transdermal patches that are available. They are discreet, low dose, and can help with a wide range of issues. I have often recommended the CBD patches for those who have anxiety about flying, or for those who need a longer relief period than flower or edibles; THC, 1:1's, and other combos are available as well. They are basically nicotine patches, but for cannabis. These little beauties can give anywhere from eight to ten hours of consistent, low dose medicine, and are to be placed on places where your skin is the thinnest.

Placement should be on the top of the foot, inside of the wrist, or even on the underside of your arm. This last one is less than desirable due to the fact that the adhesive can be super strong, so it can hurt when you peel it off. The strength of the adhesive is also something to consider when looking to use it on bruised, or paper-thin skin. Another attribute that I like about this method of intake is the fact that if the effects are too strong, or not what you were looking for, you can simply remove the patch, and you should be back to good in under an hour. You can also cut the patches in half or quarters in order to dial in the dosage next time around.[63]

I personally use them when I get a tattoo. The last one I got was quite large on my left arm and it took over seven hours to complete it in one sitting. There is no way I could have sat for that long, under that kind of pain, without my trusty patch on the inside of my left wrist.

RECTALLY

That's right folks, cannabis can also be used for and through the back door. I have seen them used for everything from hemorrhoids to rectal cancer, and they even make them for a female's front door.

If you have ever used any type of suppository, you know how messy they can be, and those made from cannabis are no different. They are generally

just a mix of coconut oil and FECO (RSO), which is then poured into bullet-shaped molds (you can find these online) to set up in the freezer. Here in Michigan, the dispensaries could not carry them at the time, as all of our products were required to be shelf stable (meaning it couldn't require refrigeration). That being said, I have walked more than a few people through the process of how to make cannabis suppositories for themselves at home after their doctors gave them the go-ahead to try this method of intake.

The feedback from those who have used suppositories is that there is very little buzz, if any at all. Most people say it feels like your body is in a warm bath, and the most unwanted side effect is simply that they are a mess to work with. In theory this is an ideal route for getting high concentrations of cannabis into the bloodstream without being metabolized by the liver, and therefore there isn't a conversion from THC to 11-Hydroxy THC.

Butt (see what I did there), the jury is out on the bioavailability of cannabinoids making it past the membranes in the caboose. According to some of the most recent research, THC itself will not get the job done as one might think. There is a man-made compound of THC called tetrahydrocannabinol-hemisuccinate (THC-HS)[64] that is showing promise as far as absorption rates.

So, do suppositories work? Many swear that they do, and it is the only way they could tolerate the high concentrations of cannabis. A person will have a far easier time taking these high doses of cannabis through the basement as opposed to the attic.

As you continue to read you will see that I am a huge advocate of whole plant medicines and products. Imagine that you have a scoop of cannabinoids, a dollop of terpenes and a dash of flavonoids in that joint in your hand or that tincture under your tongue. When all of these botanical wonders are working together you have what is called the "entourage effect," and this is becoming more of a truth than a theory.

I have always had more questions than a four-year-old at bedtime when it comes to how cannabis works in the body. I have approached many a scientist in hopes of furthering my knowledge of the subject. But unfortunately, there are too many that carry the same up-on-a-pedestal opinion that "if you can't understand it the way I say it the first time, well, then I guess you don't deserve to have this knowledge." I've even had a few tell me that I had no right to do any research on my own, that it is best left to those with a higher education. Both of these examples still rub me the wrong way when I think about them.

So, thank goodness that there are still those who offer explanations at the layperson level. I have found that these individuals are secure enough to put aside their ego to truly help us non-STEM people understand the situation. Chuck Kreiman is one of these scientists. He had spent almost two decades in drug discovery/delivery as a medicinal chemist for some huge pharma research groups focusing on neuroscience and cardiometabolic disorders, prior to focusing on botanical medications. Once on the green side of the pharma fence, he designed and then put into practice a pretty cool delivery system for cannabinoid-based medicines, and now is the director of Indo Laboratories in Massachusetts. In short, this guy knows what he is talking about when it comes to how this plant and its compounds work, and how the human body can get the most bang for its buck. There is an ongoing argument over the idea of whole-plant synergy and whether terpenes/flavonoids really do anything with cannabinoids. In a recent post Chuck summed it up in the best way I have heard yet.

"The way I see it, cannabinoids are still the medicinal star of the show, but they are 'sticky' and poorly behaved from an ADME (ADME stands for absorption, distribution, metabolism, and excretion, and describes the disposition of a pharmaceutical compound within an organism)[65] standpoint. While individual terpenes likely contribute a flavor to the medicinal effects, their purpose is to act as a natural formulation or lubricant to allow the cannabinoids to get to their destination. Actually, terpenes acting as a cardboard boat is a better analogy.

"That boat can only hold a certain number of packages (THC/CBD) before it starts to dissolve. Once the boat or lubrication is gone, the cannabinoids go back to sticking to everything they come in contact with."

THE ENTOURAGE EFFECT

The entourage effect is the theory that cannabinoids, terpenes, and flavonoids all work better as a whole than working independently. I like to use vitamin C as an example when explaining this to others.

Let's say you are trying to get some vitamin C into your life, and you have the choice between an orange (whole plant) and a vitamin supplement (isolate). The orange is a natural source of protein, fiber, folate, calcium, potassium, in addition to over 90% of your daily requirement for vitamin C. Compare that to the supplement, which only has synthetic fillers for vitamin C to play with. Which would you choose?[66]

THE ENTOURAGE EFFECT

The entourage effect is a proposed mechanism by which cannabis compounds act synergistically to modulate the overall psychoactive effects of the plant, primarily by the action of CBD and THC.

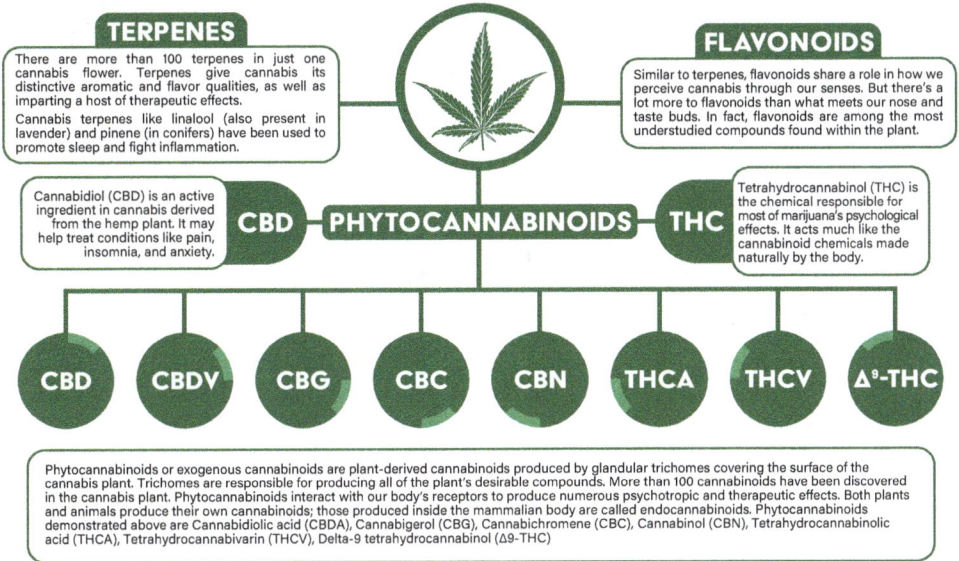

TERPENES

There are more than 100 terpenes in just one cannabis flower. Terpenes give cannabis its distinctive aromatic and flavor qualities, as well as imparting a host of therapeutic effects.

Cannabis terpenes like linalool (also present in lavender) and pinene (in conifers) have been used to promote sleep and fight inflammation.

FLAVONOIDS

Similar to terpenes, flavonoids share a role in how we perceive cannabis through our senses. But there's a lot more to flavonoids than what meets our nose and taste buds. In fact, flavonoids are among the most understudied compounds found within the plant.

Cannabidiol (CBD) is an active ingredient in cannabis derived from the hemp plant. It may help treat conditions like pain, insomnia, and anxiety.

CBD — **PHYTOCANNABINOIDS** — **THC**

Tetrahydrocannabinol (THC) is the chemical responsible for most of marijuana's psychological effects. It acts much like the cannabinoid chemicals made naturally by the body.

CBD · **CBDV** · **CBG** · **CBC** · **CBN** · **THCA** · **THCV** · **Δ⁹-THC**

Phytocannabinoids or exogenous cannabinoids are plant-derived cannabinoids produced by glandular trichomes covering the surface of the cannabis plant. Trichomes are responsible for producing all of the plant's desirable compounds. More than 100 cannabinoids have been discovered in the cannabis plant. Phytocannabinoids interact with our body's receptors to produce numerous psychotropic and therapeutic effects. Both plants and animals produce their own cannabinoids; those produced inside the mammalian body are called endocannabinoids. Phytocannabinoids demonstrated above are Cannabidiolic acid (CBDA), Cannabigerol (CBG), Cannabichromene (CBC), Cannabinol (CBN), Tetrahydrocannabinolic acid (THCA), Tetrahydrocannabivarin (THCV), Delta-9 tetrahydrocannabinol (Δ9-THC)

FULL SPECTRUM VS. BROAD SPECTRUM

You will see one of these two terms on just about every CBD product out there. But what is the difference and why does it matter?

Full spectrum means that the product has retained the full range of what was available in the beginning plant matter. These products can carry up to 0.3% of THC, along with the other cannabinoids, and has the potential to pop positive on a drug test.

Broad spectrum, also called "wide" spectrum, is when the product only has some of the plant's original properties. These products will have fewer original terpenes and cannabinoids than full spectrum. Even though these companies try really hard to ensure that zero THC is involved, it can still happen. If you are looking for something that has absolutely no chance of containing THC, isolate is the way to go, as it is straight-up pure CBD. These products are ideal for those who are sensitive to THC and/or those who are concerned about being drug tested.[67]

ISOLATES VS. WHOLE PLANT

There isn't any difference between CBD or THC that comes from hemp or marijuana. A compound is a compound. But it is the other influencing factors that can change how your body interacts with the compound.

There are several studies that back up the idea that when the cannabis plant is administered with all of its original properties intact, it not only works better, but it takes lower doses to achieve the same results as a higher-dose isolate.[68]

Of course, science needs to splice and dice individual cannabinoids and terpenes to see what they can and cannot do. But I will tell you that the minute the cannabis plant is pulled apart like this, the magic is lost. You can try to "reintroduce" terpenes and add cannabinoid isolates to the product, but it is never truly the same.

I was once sharing a meal with a cannabis processor who was very adamant that his distillate was so strong, nothing else around could compete. I of course disagreed.

I tried to have an educated discussion with him about the differences between his stripped-down THC concentrate and whole plant offerings. He wouldn't hear it. He was convinced that his 90-plus percent THC was the end-all-be-all. So, in true competitive fashion, I challenged him to try hash rosin, as it's the second strongest whole plant product on the market that you can inhale. I would've gone for the big dog FECO but that is more of an ingestion product than inhalation. I didn't want to give him any room to dispute the outcome. Technically you can smoke FECO, but my God is it harsh, and a waste of good medicine, in my opinion.

That very night he sent me a text asking what was in the product I asked him to try. "It most certainly must be laced. I have never felt anything like it," he almost whined.

I smugly responded with, "No, no. Nothing like that. What you're feeling is what happens when you keep as much of the plant together as possible. Now would you agree that even though the THC numbers have an almost 30% difference, that the hash rosin is stronger than your sweetheart distillate?" I cannot say I was surprised when, in true spoiled brat fashion, he would not concede or even acknowledge that he may have learned something new from little ol' me.

TESTING

The testing requirements for cannabis are all over the board. While some states have a laundry list of testing requirements, others waive the basic requirement to even just test products for mold. And there are some labs that report only the facts, while others will make the numbers whatever the client wants. This reminds me of my realtor days when having an appraiser in one's pocket could make the sale a bit more favorable for the client.

If you find retailers sporting plain ol' flower that "tested" out at over 35% THC, there is a really good chance that these are either the overinflated numbers of a shady testing lab, or the grower sprayed their crop with a concentrate to boost its numbers. Unfortunately, both of these deplorable actions are running rampant in our industry.

But honestly, if people didn't put so much stock in high THC potency numbers (which is nonsense), growers would not be spray tanning their incompetence all over their harvest. We have to stop feeding the high THC percentages as a good thing to our consumers. I've had 12% flower sit me down and 32 percenters do nothing but give me a headache.

> **Tip:** If someone asks for the highest THC in the place, and they don't want concentrates, stick a bug in their ear that high THC really doesn't matter. In fact, it's the other goodies in the plant and how they play with the THC that will dictate the buzz.

WHY TEST FOR TERPENES?

I am a staunch advocate for mandatory terpene testing. If you were paying attention to the preceding pages, you now know that terpenes can have all kinds of different effects on a human. By looking at a terpene test you can tell if the product will be sedative, energetic, or even carry potential allergens. Having this knowledge can reinforce your selling confidence when choosing the right cannabis variant for your customer.

> **Tip:** Something I believe to be extra important is having a binder with all of the test results available for patients to review. If you (or your vendors) are not doing anything wrong, you have nothing to hide, right? Plus, this is a great way to educate the consumer on how your Purple Punch is pretty much the same thing as your Grape Stomper.

REMEDIATION

As long as we are on the subject of questionable practices, let's talk about remediation. This technique is used to "clean up" any molds or pesticides that a grower may end up with post-harvest. I still remember the first time I saw this come across my desk. An order had come in and it was still missing the bulk flower that we had ordered several weeks ago from a too-big-for-their-britches grower. I pulled up the order in our system and saw under "testing" that their samples had failed five attempts to produce "acceptable limits" of ick. These guys just kept blasting their harvest with radiation and then resubmitting samples in hopes that the sixth time would be a charm.

The problem was described in reporting done by MLive as such: "For instance, a marijuana flower sample could fail safety testing for the presence of banned pathogens, such as E. coli, aspergillus, or salmonella; or for greater than allowed levels of heavy metals, pesticides, yeast and mold, foreign matter or water activity. The producer could then remediate and retest the product as many times as necessary. If and when it passes, labeling isn't required to contain information about the failed tests or notify the customer that product was remediated."[69]

Thankfully, there are people out there who are fighting to make any remediation public knowledge, because right now it isn't. You have no way of knowing if that joint you smoked on Friday night had been zapped over and over again in an attempt to make it safe for human consumption.

Product consistency, on the other hand, is doing much better than it was in the past. There once was a brand that made gingerbread man-shaped gummies that were notorious for both their potency and lack of homogeneity. They contained 100 mg of THC, and you never really knew what you were getting unless you ate the entire thing in one sitting. People reported when just eating an arm or a leg of the little guy they could either get nothing or found that they had consumed all 100 mgs.

This is definitely the wrong way to go when you are using cannabis as medicine. Much like how your favorite brand of blue jeans don't need to be tried on with every new pair because you know exactly how they will fit, we should have the same expectations with our cannabis products.

Product consistency and lab testing wasn't always a thing. But at one particular shop that actually did care about the well-being of its patients, there was a policy that the initial batch had to be tested before it was decided if the product would make the cut or not. Once they passed the first test, however, the processors pretty much just ran with the same procedure assuming it would all come out the same. This was most definitely not always the case.

Cannabis Carl was a well-known vendor for a very popular edible brand back in the day. Their hippy bars were notorious for being consistent, affordable, and having edibles that didn't even taste like weed. A few days after their delivery, Cannabis Carl came bursting through the front door visibly freaked out and headed straight for the offices on the second floor. First reactions were that he overcharged the big guy or screwed up the order somehow. Although not too far off, the ripple effect was an education in itself.

One of the budtenders religiously ate a 150 mg hippy bar every morning before her shift. It was her medicine, so who was I to judge? But on this day, Tina was an absolute mess. As she made her way to the break room to ride out the buzz, everybody racked their brains to try and understand what could've happened. Knowing her tolerance was way up there, it was assumed something else had gone into the mix. Seeing the popular vendor descend the steps from the offices above at that exact moment made collective light bulbs go off above everyone's heads. "What did you do Carl? What did you do to Tina?" the manager asked accusingly. Sweaty in his panic he said, "Get them off the shelf! All of them! Give me every last hippy bar that you have right now!"

It turned out the complacent kitchen staff had accidentally doubled the THC concentration to 300 mgs per bar in that particular batch. Unfortunately for Carl, he found this out the hard way when delivering the famous treats to a shop in Detroit and found that the exact same reaction had happened to some very, very large and very angry business owners. The difference between the two locations was that these guys actually threatened Carl's well-being because of the mistake, leaving him lucky to get out of there unscathed. Phoning it in can be a very real danger to both personal safety and your health in this business folks.

PEOPLE

> "Educating the mind without educating the heart is no education at all.
> **ARISTOTLE**

OUR ENDOCANNABINOID SYSTEM & CANNABIS

You have probably asked yourself at some point how cannabis can possibly work for such a broad range of medical conditions. In the age of very targeted treatments within our healthcare system, anything that claims to help more than a couple of symptoms at once is questioned. I myself even called bullshit on the vast medicinal implications of this plant. This is before I really got into the biological research surrounding cannabis, of course.

Even though cannabis has been around for a very long time, our knowledge about how and why it works in the human body didn't really get a close, hard look until the structure of the most popular phytocannabinoid, THC, was isolated by Mechoulam and Gaoni in 1964. This discovery spurred developments in the research of the Endocannabinoid System (ECS).[70]

Every single one of us has an ECS—even our pets have one. Our bodies naturally produce endocannabinoids to interact with certain receptors, and it has been discovered that the cannabis plant, which produces phytocannabinoids, has a structural similarity to these natural molecules that can stimulate the exact same receptors. This has led to a popular theory that an endocannabinoid deficiency could be the culprit of many medical conditions.

Think of your ECS as a regulator, a mother duck whose job is to keep all her ducklings on track. One of the reasons the cannabis plant can potentially aid in such a wide range of conditions is because it interacts with all of our internal systems. If your nervous system is firing way too hot, your ECS may tell it to calm down. If your immune system is sluggish and unproductive, your ECS may tell it to get up off its tush and do its job. Our ECS keeps track of these ducklings as they wander off or fall behind and brings them back into the fully functioning fold.

ENDOCANNABINOID SYSTEM

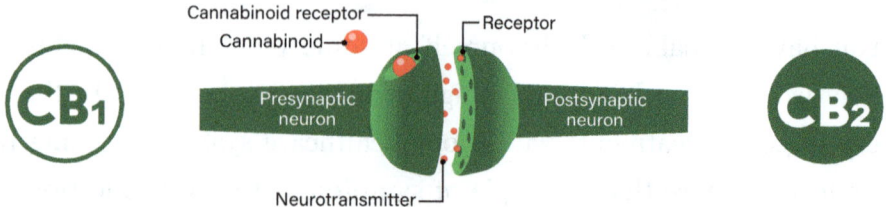

CB1

- Peripheral nervous system
- Central nervous system
- Brain and spinal cord
- Digestive tract
- Pituitary gland
- Thyroid gland
- Adrenal gland
- Muscle cells
- Liver cells
- Fat cells
- Placenta
- Ovaries
- Kidneys
- Retinas
- Lungs
- Sperm

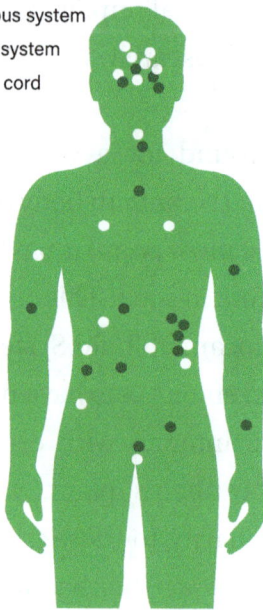

CB2

- Peripheral nervous system
- Reproductive system
- Adipose tissue
- Digestive tract
- Thymus gland
- Bone marrow
- Immune cells
- Pancreas
- Kidneys
- Spleen
- Tonsils
- Bones
- Brain
- Liver
- Skin
- Eyes

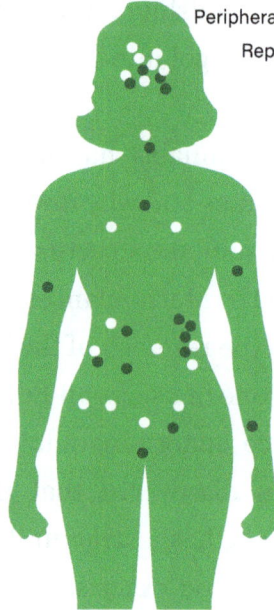

The two most popular cannabinoid receptors in current research are the CB1 and CB2. Some of the CB1 receptors are located in the brain, spinal cord, lungs, and kidneys, just to name a few. The CB2 receptors can be found in the immune system, spleen, liver cells, and the nervous system. As research evolves every day, we are finding more and more interactions with these receptors.

According to Dr. Peter Grinspoon from Harvard Medical School, "The cannabinoid receptors in the brain—the CB1 receptors—outnumber many of the other receptor types on the brain. They act like a traffic cop to control the levels and activity of most of the other neurotransmitters.

"A second type of cannabinoid receptor, the CB2 receptor, exists mostly in our immune tissues and is critical to helping control our immune functioning, and it plays a role in modulating intestinal inflammation, contraction, and pain in inflammatory bowel conditions. CB2 receptors are particularly exciting targets of drug development because they don't cause the high associated with cannabis that stimulating the CB1 receptors does (which is often an unwanted side effect)."[71]

In review, any cannabinoid that pokes the CB1 receptor will have some intoxicating effects. However, if the CB2 receptor is provoked, you will not get that intoxication reaction. And stimulating both of the receptors at the same time can lead to yet another experience. So, knowing which cannabinoids and/or cannabinoid terpene combos interact with which receptors, and how they interact, may just give us some of the answers we have been looking for when it comes to using botanical medicine.

THE MOST COMMON POSITIVE SIDE EFFECTS

After years of feedback from the legions of patients that have crossed my path, three of the most popular positive side effects from cannabis are solid sleep, general relaxation, and movement in their pipes. The first two may not surprise you, as cannabis is well-known for these qualities. But the last one was something I hadn't considered until people began to really speak openly about their cannabis use.

We all know that one of the most common side effects of taking pharmaceuticals is constipation. But some people found that as they used cannabis to either wean off or supplement their medications, they began to consistently take the Browns to the Super Bowl again.

THE MOST COMMON NEGATIVE SIDE EFFECTS

ALLERGIC REACTIONS

As we all know, introducing nature into our lives can be both a blessing and a curse—just ask anyone with seasonal allergies. A person can absolutely have an allergic reaction to cannabis.

Cannabis does not have to interact with other substances, such as prescribed drugs, to be harmful. Whether suffering a reaction from constantly overindulging in THC, or reacting to certain terpenes, allergic side effects from consuming cannabis are a possibility. "Linalool is a major constituent of cannabis and can be a very weak allergen if an allergic reaction occurs at all. However, linalool autoxidizes on air exposure, and the oxidation products can cause contact allergy. If a person who develops an allergy to these byproducts inhales linalool via concentrates, a strong anaphylaxis, or systemic allergic reaction which includes the familiar symptoms of hyperventilation, hives, and itchiness, can likewise occur."[72]

So even though most of us will feel a calming sensation from encountering lavender in nature, inhaling it in concentrated form at high temperatures can be totally different, and sometimes will have harmful outcomes.

A person really has to be aware of their own bodies and heed the warnings. If you know that you are allergic or sensitive to dairy, you scan labels to ensure that you won't be doing yourself in, right? The same line of thinking has to go into any natural airborne allergies that might be present, as the very same terpenes that are found in these plants can also be found in cannabis, especially when smoking or vaporizing flower or concentrates.

This is yet another reason why terpene testing should be mandatory at the state level, especially in the medical markets. When you find yourself interacting with a new-to-cannabis consumer or someone who reports allergy-like symptom complaints, flat out ask them if they have seasonal allergies. The fix could be as simple as steering them away from pinene and toward limonene.

CANNABINOID HYPEREMESIS SYNDROME (CHS)

CHS is fairly new and is confusing both the medical community and the consumer. There is a very spirited, ongoing debate about the actual cause of this affliction and diagnosing it properly. Some swear that it is caused by crappy growing processes, including monstrous pesticides and fertilizers being sprayed directly on the plant as well as added to the soil. Others are looking at it from a scientific point of view because pesticide poisoning doesn't present the same symptoms as CHS.

> "Cannabinoid Hyperemesis Syndrome is characterized by chronic cannabis use, cyclic episodes of nausea and vomiting, and frequent hot bathing. Cannabinoid Hyperemesis Syndrome occurs by an unknown mechanism."[73]

These side effects are also different from those reported from overdoing it with edibles. In fact, many of the effects of CHS can be absent for years (especially if a person abused cannabis as an adolescent), and then rear its ugly head once a person begins to indulge in cannabis again. According to the study quoted above, not only THC, but CBD and CBG, may also play a role in CHS.

There are recent studies that show there is a genetic predisposition for it[74] and to confuse things even further, there are too many ER doctors who are misdiagnosing it as Cyclic Vomiting Syndrome and as a result treating it wrong. CHS is a great example of the work that still needs to be done on the research front with cannabis consumption.

DRUG INTERACTIONS

While we are still on the subject of the negatives of cannabis, let's discuss the reality of cannabis and drug interactions.

Cannabis does have drug interactions. Please understand this statement.

We have been so conditioned to leaving this up to our doctors and pharmacists that most of us will not take the time to look into it ourselves. We most definitely do not have this luxury when it comes to cannabis. This interaction can cause a drug to be far less or way more potent than intended, and it is up to you, the consultant, to bring this to the attention of the newbie. Of course, beyond this warning personal responsibility comes into play to ensure that they are doing everything they can to protect themselves.

A very basic way to know if current (and future) pharmaceuticals will have an interaction with cannabis is to watch for a "grapefruit warning" on the pill bottles. This sour citrus dances with the same metabolizing liver enzyme that we had spoken about earlier in regard to edibles. "Grapefruit juice decreases the activity of the cytochrome P450 3A4 (CYP3A4) enzymes that are responsible for breaking down many drugs and toxins."[75] Some may think that you would have to drink gallons of the stuff in order for it to have an effect. Think again.

> "One whole fruit or 200 milliliters of grapefruit juice (a bit less than one cup) can block the CYP3A4 enzymes and lead to toxic blood levels of the drug."[76]

Blood thinners and medications for epilepsy are famous for having this warning attached to their bottles. Let's say that they have been taking the same drug for years to keep their seizures at bay, and it's working, but they would like to try to introduce cannabis into their healthcare regimen.

The very last thing they want is to start having seizures again because you didn't do your due diligence by informing the customer. Cannabis also interacts with anesthesia, making it less effective. If it happens to come up that the person you are helping is planning on surgery in the future, please be sure to drop this little nugget of information in their ear. From a management standpoint, I'm a big fan of the idea of putting up a sign in the lobby that issues this warning just in case they're not picking up what you're laying down.

There is an available search engine to check if a certain medication interacts with cannabis. I have not been given permission to add the actual link, so I will tell you to search Penn State's website (wink).

> Tip: If the customer isn't sure, you can suggest that they ask their doctor if any newly proposed medications carry this warning prior to them prescribing it. The conversation with the doctor could go something like this: "I would like to start you on ABC medication for your migraines," the doctor says. They can respond with, "Does ABC come with a grapefruit warning? I use CBD and I know it carries the same warnings as a grapefruit interaction."

DRUG TESTING – ON THE JOB AND ON THE ROAD

One of the most common questions retailers get is, "Will I pass a drug test if I'm just taking CBD?" Let us think back to the explanation of spectrums vs. isolates in CBD products. If your CBD gummies or tincture are either broad, wide, or full spectrums, there is always the possibility of trace amounts of THC and therefore the potential to pop hot on a test. But if your chosen product is made with isolates, then I'd say you're pretty safe.

"According to Quest Diagnostics Director of Science and Technology, Barry Sample, CBD likely won't show up on a drug test: 'If the product contains only CBD and has had the THC removed, then an individual being tested would not be expected to test positive for marijuana or marijuana metabolite.' In other words, marijuana drug tests screen for THC, not CBD."[77]

Now when it comes to mandatory drug tests, many cry foul when a company requires THC drug testing using the argument of local legality. After all, they don't care if you have beers on the weekend, or an open script for heavy painkillers, as long as you can do your job without risk to the company or your fellow employees. Yet when it comes to marijuana, even if you are a medical marijuana card holder, there is often a hard line in the sand against it. And for the most part, for good reason.

Would you want your surgeon stoned before your operation? Do you want that gravel-hauler driver who shares the road with you all grassed up? Would you want your babysitter high watching your terrible-two toddler? I think not.

But there is also a flip side. That surgeon may take a low dose edible before bed to ensure he is properly rested. That truck driver may take a few drops of a CBD tincture that has a splash of THC in it for his bad back. That babysitter may take a microdose as a part of her morning regimen to combat anxiety instead of the tweaker Adderall. None of these examples will render these professionals stoned, and they are using cannabis as medicine—responsibly.

There are so many varying degrees of "intoxication" when it comes to cannabis. You may be someone who occasionally takes a gummy to help shut your head off at night and by morning you only feel well rested. And then there are those who huff on a vape pen all day, every day. Both of these examples will pop hot on a drug test. Because THC is stored in our fat cells, cannabis will hang around in our system much, much longer than the buzz does.

Ex: You enjoy a few cocktails over Labor Day weekend and the thought of failing a roadside sobriety test on the following Tuesday just isn't realistic. But if you smoke a joint on the same weekend and are subjected to a roadside swab on the way to dropping your kids off at school three weeks later, you will fail the test. So, even though the buzz is long gone, you are now being charged with driving while intoxicated and child endangerment.

The type of test, how often, and how much THC you use, has a lot to do with how long you will be coming in hot on a drug test.

"Research on the amount of time a test can detect cannabis shows a wide range of averages. Research from 2017 estimates a detection window for a single cannabis cigarette of about 3 days."[78]

The same study emphasizes that detection windows vary and depend on how often a person smokes.

It showed:
- For someone smoking cannabis for the first time, tests may detect it for about 3 days.
- In someone who smokes cannabis three or four times per week, the detection window is 5–7 days.
- For people who smoke cannabis once a day or more, tests may detect it in their system for 30 days or longer.

Detection windows also depend on the kind of test a person undertakes. General estimates for various cannabis tests are as follows:
- Urine tests can detect cannabis in the urine for approximately 3–30 days after use.
- Saliva tests can detect cannabis for approximately 24 hours after use. Some saliva tests have detected cannabis for up to 72 hours.
- Hair tests are the most sensitive tests, detecting THC for up to 90 days after use. However, these tests are testing the oil in skin that transfers to hair, and so they may occasionally show a false positive. A person who comes into contact with a THC user could, theoretically, test positive on a hair test.
- Blood tests can only detect THC for 3–4 hours.

Technology and science must catch up sooner rather than later when it comes to cannabis intoxication. It is imperative that testing for marijuana, roadside or not, be as precise as other impairment tests. People are still having their lives ruined by inaccurate drug testing, and it has to stop. As it stands now, positive test results do not equal intoxication. Read that again.

But if you are someone who likes to brag that you are a better driver when stoned: you are a part of the problem, you deserve the ticket. Nobody should ever, ever drive under the influence of anything that alters your cognition or your reaction time.

PETS

We all love our fur babies and would do pretty much anything to ease any of their suffering. All animals have an endocannabinoid system, just as we do, but the difference is that our pets break down and distribute cannabinoids differently.

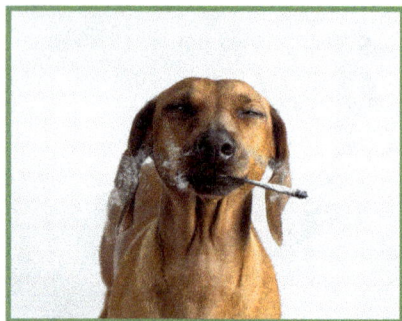

Dogs don't do great with consuming THC. Whether they are given this intoxicating compound intentionally, or they got into your stash, it can put your pooch in a bad way. Because dogs have way more CB1 receptors than their humans do, they are prone to "static ataxia," which is defined by the medical dictionary as "a loss of deep sensibility, causing the inability to preserve equilibrium in standing."[79] In English, this means they will stumble around, or may even be unable to get themselves up on their own four paws, much like a drunken sailor, with doses of THC as low as 0.5 mgs.[80] Yet studies are showing that your pets can safely tolerate much higher levels of CBD. These studies also bring attention to the oils that these cannabinoids are offered in, as they are often the culprit for any stomach distress.[81, 82]

If you believe that Fido has gotten into your edibles, the following signs may be used to confirm whether you should get him to the vet ASAP.

THE MOST COMMON SIGNS OF EXCESS CANNABIS EXPOSURE IN DOGS AND CATS

NEUROLOGICAL
- SLEEPINESS
- ATAXIA

DEPRESSION
- WOBBLING, PACING AND AGITATION
- VOCALIZATION

EYES
- DILATED PUPILS
- BLOODSHOT EYES

GASTRO-INTESTINAL
- VOMITING
- SALIVATION

OTHERS
- SOUND OR LIGHT SENSITIVITY
- LOW BODY TEMPERATURE
- INAPPROPRIATE URINATION
- FAST OR SLOW HEART RATES

POLICY

> " What a way to run a railroad.
>
> **BUGS BUNNY**

DISCLAIMER

I loved my time in cannabis retail! Yes, the hours were long, and the work was physically and mentally challenging. But no two day were the same, I adored (most of) my co-workers, and I was always learning something new. There isn't quite anything like the rush of looking around the store under your control and seeing that the place is packed, knowing your staff is an intelligent, well-oiled rig, and that people are happy.

The following policy experiences and opinions come from my work in the medical cannabis retail arena. But these lessons and suggestions can and absolutely should be applied to adult-use businesses. Some states have had hundreds of thousands of medical cannabis patients prior to opening up with adult use. Reports from all over the country will show you how the medical card holder numbers fall through the floor once rec passes. But it's not like all of the med patients just ceased to exist. There are still those massive groups, it's just that they prefer not to be on "the list" when it comes to their cannabis consumption. So, even if your location and/or products are deemed "recreational" or "adult use," keep in mind that all cannabis is medicinal.

I have learned, sometimes painfully, that you simply cannot be prepared for every situation that walks into a pot shop. Humans are still so widely unpredictable that even after more than a decade of working behind the cannabis retail counter, I was still surprised almost every day. One of the best things you can do for your company, your staff, and yourself, is to pay attention and learn from the "Well, that sucked. Let's not have that happen again" events. Change that expensive standard operating procedure. Modify that membership agreement. Listen, I mean seriously listen to the employees who are on the front lines of your business. As the saying goes, "Adapt or die."

PRODUCT KNOWLEDGE

I know brands out there will argue, after all they have spent heavy coin to get in front of the consumer, but to be successful you should above all want to be helpful. It has been said that in sales you should "sell the problem it solves, not the product." This is beyond true in the cannabis space.

Getting to know the products you carry inside and out will not only help your patients, but also increase the cannabis intelligence of your budtenders. Make no mistake, your patients are paying attention. They know that the orange ABC gummies tested out higher this time around than the cherry. Do you? Every time a new order comes in the door, check out the test results specific to that batch. You may have been ordering this brand for months, but each batch can vary.

Cannabinoid content is just as important as the manufacturing process (e.g., is it distillate or whole plant?) and so is the integrity of the company behind the brand.

So many of us choose sides every day. Some refuse to shop at certain grocery stores because of the treatment of their staff, while others will boycott another retailer due to their political beliefs. So why shouldn't it be the same in cannabis? Is it because some brands and their dirty laundry are not plastered all over the evening news? Or is it because to buy marijuana legally is still a novel privilege and some people just want their product to be cheap and effective? I'd say it's a little column A and a little column B.

I say we take "branding" out of the conversation. If your product is really the cat's pajamas, it won't need flashy packaging or celebrity endorsements. Budtenders everywhere will always push what works for them, regardless of the fancy swag you dole out on vender days.

Once we had a vendor day with a company that quite honestly had a garbage product. They came with bright banners, a buy three get the fourth for free enticement, and even vape batteries engraved with each budtenders name. Yes, it brought in a slightly bigger crowd, but the staff knew better.

Their carts were famous for leaking, containing heavy cutting agents, and always tasted like perfume. Not a single budtender bought the carts to go with their newly monogrammed batteries.

PACKAGING

I don't think anyone would argue that the packaging in cannabis is out of control. We get it. It is to make them child-proof, but a pill or booze bottle is far, far easier to get into than some of this stuff. And I won't address the very real issue of the kind of waste it is producing (for now) but stay focused on how it affects the consumer.

The majority of cannabis products are wrapped and sealed in such a way that you almost always need scissors to get into your purchase. And when you are using these products for medical reasons it can get beyond frustrating just trying to get to what will ease your pain.

As a floor manager I would have empty packaging available, including mylar bags, dube tubes and concentrate jars, to show people how they are to be opened. You may get the "do I look stupid" stare, but especially with new consumers, they may not know how difficult it can truly be.

DELI STYLE

There is an ongoing debate on whether deli style (loose in a jar) or pre-packed is the best way to go when it comes to selling cannabis flower. Some side with the pre-packed for the security of it being sealed and less risk of contamination. While others (like me) prefer the deli style so your nose and eyes can do the shopping. There are two grave errors a budtender can make when working with deli style. The first is shaking up the jar before opening it for the customer to smell. This may wake up the terpenes, but it's also beating the hell out of them, and you will end up with less potent buds and a ton more kief at the bottom of the jar, which most likely will be wasted.

The second, and most blasphemous in my opinion, is breaking a beautiful bud in half just so you can get the weight correct on your scale. Please stop. It's painful to watch. Instead, fish around in the jar for a smaller bud to get to your weight. Otherwise, you will just end up with half broken buds at the bottom of the jar, which is ugly and harder to sell.

MANAGING YOUR PHYSICAL SPACE

Not everyone has the opportunity to build their retail location from scratch. The majority have to take what they can get given strict zoning issues, regardless of what state you are in. You simply have to get in where you fit in. Out of the five dispensaries that I have worked at, a few were old houses converted into a commercial space and came with some challenges regarding the functionality. These converted homes had steep steps leading to the front door and suck-in-your-gut narrow doorways once inside. At one place the door guy, and whatever strong staff member they could find, would have to carry the patient's wheelchair up the stairs and squeeze it through the doorway. These patients and their chairs couldn't make it through the second doorway, which led to the med room. A budtender would have to run back and forth showing products to the patient.

In another location they had a ramp out back, but once inside, the patient found himself in the back inventory room and would have to navigate their way into the med room from behind the counter. This setup was completely against the law, as no one who was not an employee or approved vendor was allowed access to the area.

Now, how awful is this for the patient! The Americans with Disabilities Act is there for a reason folks. People with wheelchairs, walkers, crutches, and canes, have every right to be able to access storefronts, and not through the back door or left in the lobby like third-class citizens.

And regrettably more and more retail locations run a system where you will speak with a budtender to place the order and then you are shoved into what I call a cow corral to wait in line to pay for your purchase. There isn't a chair to be found for those who cannot stand in line for long periods of time.

These obstacles can be overcome with some creative thinking. It can be as simple as putting a rug over a threshold for easier rolling and less of a tripping hazard. Or it can be as big as opening up a doorway, changing stairs into a ramp, or adding double handrails. Another way you can accommodate your customers is by keeping chairs and a wheelchair available for anyone who may need them. Cannabis compassion is more than just shoveling the snow from the walkway.

People in general really don't need much to profess their loyalty to a company. I have found that honesty and transparency will secure their homage. You really don't have to spend too much time or money on these efforts either. I have seen countless approaches to make yourself stand out from the rest in attempts to retain their customer base. Some were as novel as spinning a carnival wheel to see what percentage got knocked off their bill, to offering to roll a joint on the spot with any of the flower on the shelves. This one was a bit counterproductive to the patient flow, in my opinion. A budtender had to stop what they were doing, weigh out the gram, grind it up and hand roll the joint while others were waiting in line just to be seen. If you have ever worked in the restaurant business, I can compare this to someone asking for a hand-squeezed pitcher of lemonade during the dinner rush.

Tip: I know you can't always control the temperature of your show room, but you can be mindful of the heat coming off of the lighting in your display cases. Products cooking under those lights all day can and will degrade the potency of those products, should you plan to sell them at a discount at a later date.

WHO TO HIRE
(WITH OR WITHOUT EXPERIENCE)

When staffing a retail cannabis establishment, recognize that you are, in fact, building an army. Your hires should include communications, intelligence, muscle, and of course, special forces.

Your hand-picked staff will be the boots on the ground of your retail operation. Understanding that not all situations can be successfully managed by traditional methods will be a major key to your success. Dealing with product refunds and state-sanctioned purchasing limits will require more than just good guidelines; you'll need staff with the skills to actually execute them in real time.

So, instead of hiring those who are only in it because it would be cool to sling weed, staff your business with your own medical condition specialists. One should be an ace in anxiety, another a devil dog of depression, and another a decorated captain of chronic pain, as these are the most common conditions that will cross your threshold.

Employees with firsthand knowledge of suffering from these conditions themselves, or having loved ones who do, will reinforce your reputation with your patients and strengthen the confidence in their care. These life-experienced personnel, when strategically placed, create your own unique synergy, your own entourage effect, if you will.

A consultant who suffers with anxiety themselves can confidently and honestly recommend what cannabis products work, or don't work, for them personally. These conversations, on a shared condition and with firsthand experiences, will create a bond of true understanding. The healing process for a patient seems a bit less daunting, a little less lonely, knowing that someone else has been where they are now. It is these kinds of connections that are a dispensary's biggest staffing asset in retaining patient loyalty.

At one point, I had worked with a fantastic consultant who had unfortunately been in a tragic car accident, which put her into a wheelchair. Her upbeat look at life, and visibly obvious personal knowledge of what it means to be in pain, had patients waiting in line to be specifically seen by her. They knew she could relate and was on top of the latest and greatest cannabis products available for relentless chronic pain.

Taking advice from someone who has never lived day in and day out with the mental struggles that come with physical pain, or the physical side effects from mental anguish, is like having a dietitian who doesn't care for cake. They can explain the textbook science behind why your body craves sweets, but that's where it ends. They can sympathize, but never really understand the place you are coming from.

I have also always believed having veterans in our ranks not only employs our honorable service men and women, but they also share an unspoken bond with others who have served. Whether it is—what seems like to most of us—coded language and inside jokes, or just a look and a nod, there is a healing comradery in the time they spend together. The fact that their service may have been decades and oceans apart has little bearing. The veterans on staff can recommend medication without verbally pushing a private veteran into dumping their emotional baggage out on the counter. These relations are worth their weight in gold. Not only to the establishment and its reputation, but more importantly, the well-being of the patient.

MINORS AND THEIR CAREGIVERS

There seems to be an all-out panic that runs through a shop when a minor is in the lobby. We have been so conditioned that cannabis is the devil's lettuce, and we must "save the children," that we forget that sometimes a child is in fact the patient.

Make no mistake, cannabis, in any form, should be locked up just like your liquor cabinet or your prescriptions for the safety of everyone involved. But when the proper steps have been taken by a parent to legally register their child as a medical marijuana patient, it is safe to say that they are only there as a last-ditch effort to help their kid.

When the regulated medical market started in Michigan, everyone was so skittish that they seemed to have forgotten the caregiver laws that had been in place since 2008. Under this law, in order for a minor to receive the blessings of the state for medical cannabis, they have to have two separate recommendations.

One from their pediatrician and one from another doctor. A parent also must be tied to them as their caregiver. Assuming all of this was on the up and up, both the parent and the minor were allowed into marijuana retail shops. Yet the higher-ups would become unglued when they saw these couples in the lobby. I have experienced this a few times, but the one that really sticks was one where I had to defend a young man who had the exact same rare disease that I do.

The receptionist called me to the front to double-check on the legality of a mother and minor looking to come in, and after seeing that everything was in order, I allowed them into the med room. Not ten seconds later, one of the higher-ups came flying into the room and made a beeline for me and the mother and son at the counter. "He can't be in here! He's clearly underage so we can't sell him anything. He HAS to go now!" Having been shamed, the mother and son began to move away from the counter to leave.

"Stop," I said with visible embarrassment for the ignorance of the boss. "Let me see your cards again," I asked the mom. Laying the cards next to each other on the counter for inspection, I replied, "Yep. Both cards are valid and unexpired.

"Under our caregiver laws this young man is well within his rights to be in here as long as he is accompanied by his caregiver, which is this patient lady standing in front of you." Because he was made to look like the ass that he was, he snapped back with, "I'd feel a lot better if she left him in the car and just made the purchase herself." Mind you this was a sixteen-year-old boy that he was treating like a toddler.

"Why shouldn't this young man be allowed to learn about the medicine he's taking? Do you have any idea how useful this information would have been for me when I was young? He needs to know this stuff for when he turns eighteen and starts going to these places by himself," I clapped back. Not another word came out of the higher-up's mouth as he slinked away from the unnecessary altercation with his ego tucked between his legs.

I apologized to both of them for the interruption and continued with the consultation. Learning that the teenager had the exact same disability that I did really helped with my recommendations (and warnings), and today I still feel like I did my job to the fullest extent, my superiors be damned. I not only stood up for the duo, but I also gave them a sounding board who made them feel we knew what they were going through.

COVERING YOUR BASES WHEN CATERING TO PATIENTS

Some retail locations are placed to cater to assisted living facilities in the area. I worked in one such location where it was common that residents would use their motorized scooters to come by for their medication. They would leave their transportation on the back stoop where they could plug it in for a quick charge while they were shopping. It seemed to work pretty well for everyone involved, until it didn't.

Hank came to see us every Thursday and knew the routine. What he failed to mention is that his scooter had been on the fritz and was struggling to hold a charge. So even though we had plugged in his ride, the thing wouldn't start when he had finished shopping. I wasn't really sure how to handle the situation with Hank in my wheeled office chair and his dead horse. After being informed that there wasn't anyone to come to get him, as his housing complex didn't run shuttles on Thursdays, I called him an Uber on my dime. While we waited, I tried to get in touch with the facility to let them know that we had his scooter and that we could keep it overnight, if need be, but that was the absolute extent that we could keep it in the shop. My call was not met with much concern for Hank and his horse, only a "We'll see what we can do." Though this response was not helpful at the time, it taught me to ask these patients for an emergency contact number to add to their patient profile in case things went sideways.

WORDS MATTER

I don't believe that there is a single medical state that went adult use and didn't see its registered patient numbers drop. Here in Michigan, we had over 300 thousand registered patients and caregivers the day before we went rec. Five years later we have less than 50 thousand. Why? Did they all just stop using cannabis or move out of state? Hardly. These people are still at our counters, it's just that they now have the option to not be forced onto "a list."

Suzy still uses gummies to calm her mind, and Jack still has that bad hip that likes to sing when the weather gets damp. So why did those behind the counter stop treating them like the medical patients that they are?

I personally believe it comes down to the in-house training. Budtenders are conditioned from day one to focus on what's popular and which brands are paying the guys upstairs to push their product. It seems we have gone from "offerings" to "the hard sell" and it is doing more harm than good.

I enjoy doing recon at different shops not only to see what they have going on, but to see how the budtender handles the consult (or these days, the sale). A good example to make my point here was when I went into a former medical store turned rec. The first statement out of the budtender's mouth was, "Do you know what you want?" Since I always ask for something that is more medicinal than an infused pre-roll, I answered with, "I'm actually looking for a 1:1 chocolate bar." After a glazed moment, which I gave her the benefit of the doubt was not because she didn't know what I meant but was just running through their inventory in her head. "No, but we have 1:1 CBN gummies for sleep." She walked me over to the display and pointed out an option. I told her I was really hoping for something a bit "meltier" and asked if she had a tincture with the ratio I was looking for (I had spotted one when I walked in). She didn't move. She came back with, "We also have these gummies for sleep." Getting irritated I told her, "I never said it was for sleep." Now she was irritated. With a huff she came back with, "Well then I can't help you ma'am."

What should have this undereducated budtender done differently?

For starters, had she asked me "What brings you in?" instead of "Do you know what you want?" I would've been more forthcoming about what I was going to use the product for. Instead, she just assumed that it was for sleep and then got frustrated when it wasn't. Who knows, maybe I looked more tired than I thought that day. Also, a lot of newbies looking to use cannabis as medicine don't really know what they are looking for, they just know what they are trying to treat. A budtender can figure out pretty quick with just that one introductory question whether the person is there for medical reasons or for recreational.

This lovely lady also could've asked for ideas or assistance from a co-worker to try and help me out. At least I would've felt like they were making an effort. Now, had I packed the patience to make this a teaching moment, I would have asked for someone else and then promptly pointed out the tincture on the other side of the room. Instead, I took my happy ass out the door and down the road.

THE HARD SELL

A popular complaint about cannabis retail is the feeling of being "sold." That the person you are paired with has no higher goal than to make their number or to dump as much of the Monday morning push product as possible. Nobody, and I mean nobody, likes to be upsold. It's a huge turnoff and your customer can sense it. The "Hey man, I got the highest THC right here for you" has got to stop. Cannabis should not be approached like used car sales or extended warranties, although with the text pushes, it's encroaching on the latter. Focusing solely on the bottom dollar and not why the patron is at your store in the first place is giving you a bad name and it's killing the compassionate nature of the cannabis culture.

Once upon a time, I had a very sales number driven employee, even though there wasn't an incentive at this particular shop to be "top in sales." Marion came positively bursting into my office one afternoon with the news that she had just made a three-thousand-dollar sale. "My goodness that's a big bill! What did they buy?" I had asked. As Marion plopped down in a chair, very proud of herself, she said "it was all RSO." I was instantly disgusted by her behavior. "Happy to profit off of the sick" was sitting directly in front of me in flesh and blood. My disdain quickly turned to dread knowing what was coming out of my mouth next and how it would be received. I went scorched earth on Marion.

"What in the hell is wrong with you? How can you be happy about someone buying three grand in RSO? Do you have any idea how sick someone has to be to spend that kind of cash on what is most likely a last-ditch effort before someone dies?" I chastised.

I still regret how it happened as I tell you this story. Marion definitely learned this alternative point of view of her cash cow sale without kindness or professionalism. I had failed us both. I now always make it a point to tell others that high sales of RSO is never a good thing and should be treated with respect for the situation. Marion also changed her demeanor to sincerity instead of sales numbers when the customer returned to make the same purchase the following month. Managing is hard.

SERVICE ANIMAL POLICY

Of course, we all love a service dog. What's not to like? They're smart, well behaved, and are helping a human in need. Granted, things got a bit out of hand there for a minute with some emotional support animals. A peacock, really? I am glad these people have found something to help with their trials but having them in a public space can sometimes be problematic.

The shops I have worked at all had some sort of policy regarding these furry companions. We would keep a bowl of fresh water outside for them on hot days, and even hemp treats behind the counter for when they visited with their humans. But unfortunately, sometimes the situation calls for what is in the best interest for patients as a whole, and not just the individual.

Once we had a woman come in with a purse pooch under her arm without any certification or service animal documents that would accommodate our policy. Yet nonetheless she was allowed entry by reception and proceeded to plop that puppy right on the glass top of one of our display cases.

So, I kindly asked her to either keep the dog in her arms or on the floor. You would think that I was threatening to take the mutt if she did not comply with the way she reacted. "Don't you DARE touch her!" she yelled while snatching the animal off the glass. "She has every right to be here! Just like I do!" the woman boasted. Trying to calm both the situation and my expression, I explained that in fact the dog had zero privileges due to the lack of paperwork, and that she never should have made it into the room because of this. And before she could spew more of her fantasy rights, I told her that having the dog on the actual counter was what I had an issue with. "Why? She isn't hurting anything!" the woman whined. I was losing my patience with this woman who couldn't see any farther than the tip of her own surgically sculpted nose.

"Because some people can have allergies to dogs, ma'am. And not only that, but medicine is also dispensed over this counter. It's not very sanitary to have a dog on the counter. You are not our only patient, and we pride ourselves on a safe and clean environment for everyone who visits."

With a snarky "my dog is not dirty," she was passed off to a budtender for a consultation. She was also reminded again on her way out that next time the dog would not be allowed into the med room without proper documentation. I headed for the receptionist to deliver a speech about how the situation never should have happened, and why we had the policies that we did.

SECURITY

Anyone who has ever walked into a pot shop can clearly see that every square inch of the place is being monitored by cameras. As it should be. These locations have a deeper concern for the possibility of being knocked over than, say, a liquor store. If a party store is robbed it's usually for the cash, lottery tickets, and smokes. The thieves are not looking to snag booze-based inventory because there generally isn't a resale demand. You are not likely to find the sale of individual shots of vodka on the street corners any time soon (I'd hope). But with cannabis, the bandit can easily break it down and distribute it.

Having had marijuana illegal for so long, we have all been conditioned to the idea that law enforcement are the bad guys. And in turn, I believe they have always seen us as the bad guys. Both sides have to stop thinking this way within the regulated market. Every single place that I have worked at understood that we needed to be at the very least friendly with our local law enforcement. I won't lie. It is uncomfortable at first for both sides, but neither are going anywhere, so we might as well support each other.

I encourage retail owners to invite them in! Be proud and show off your state-of-the-art beast of a safe! Brag about your key fob entry security system that you paid out your eyes for! Show them exactly what is going on and diffuse any preconceived notions of wrongdoing.

I once gave a local sheriff a tour, and I made sure to point out the age demographic in the room. They weren't degenerates or kingpins. They were middle-aged professionals looking for a bit of grease for the tin man's joints and grandparents hoping to purchase a couple of z's for the night. I also suggest that you set up some sort of an informational meet and greet with the local po-po. They can tell your staff what to expect and how to react if in fact the place is robbed or if there is a dangerous situation. Your staff in turn can let the police in on their concerns and questions when it comes to cannabis access within the shared community.

Now on the subject of employee safety, a set-in-stone policy has to be implemented. Especially in the case of delivery drivers and split shifts, your employees could be coming and going throughout the day. Requiring employees to use the buddy system is the best policy, in my opinion. Yep, it can be a pain in the ass waiting for someone to walk you out, but there is safety in numbers just in case someone is casing the joint.

SUITS VS. LEGACY

Whether you were into cannabis before regulation or not can be a pretty big bridge to cross in this industry. Those who have risked everything from parking lot deals to losing their freedom have their feet firmly planted in the history and culture of this plant. They built the table that others now want to own. Then there are those who jumped in once they saw that there was money to be made and stomped their feet toddler-style saying they are entitled to the table because they have college degrees and have run corporations. Sniveling that surely they must know the business of cannabis better than anyone else.

In the early days of regulation here in Michigan we saw the investors (suits) scoop up as many legacy growers and processors as they could to get their shiny new cannabis businesses off the ground. Once these guys built these empires for others using their years of very hard-earned experience, they were cut loose. I have personally experienced a suit trying to influence the way certain products were made by cutting corners to save a buck. When arguing with them that's not how the plant or the process works and it can actually cause harm to the consumer, I was met with the response of "Well, it's my money. I have the final say."

These battles are quite common for those of us who have worked on both sides of the regulatory fence. I was managing a newly opened shop that was actually pulling in great numbers, but the bosses decided to bring in a consultant who ran a few Apple stores in New York. I'm all for new ideas to make retail more efficient, as long as they understand that the consumer is the most important part of our business.

Cody was a great guy with great ideas. He tweaked our intake process to cut down on wait times and showed us new ways to stay organized throughout the mad rushes. But what Cody just couldn't seem to grasp is that the cannabis we were selling wasn't anything like the iPhones and tablets he pedaled out East. We were there to help others with this plant and consultations sometimes took time. It wasn't always his ideal turn and burn situation. He would say things like, "This isn't any different than selling garbage cans. It's basic sales. Get them in and move them out." Insisting that he was wrong, I asked him to take a walk with me up the street to the local drugstore.

Once strategically placed in the rear of the store I asked Cody to look around. "Now with the pharmacy counter to your left and rows of over-the-counter products on your right, would you say they are both the same products?" Speaking to him like a kindergarten teacher trying to get a child to walk through the reasoning process with me. "Of course not. The pharmacy has controlled substances that are tracked." I was hoping to see a light go off above his head, yet I found myself disappointed. "OK ... are there any differences between the person behind the counter on your left and the person behind the counter at the front of the store?" I asked patiently. "You know there is Ang. The pharmacist makes sure they know how to take the drug, answers any questions..." Cody finally saw the light! Selling cannabis is different from selling garbage cans (at least it used to be). I patted myself on the back on the walk back to the shop that I actually got a suit to see things from the legacy side of the fence.

COMMON MEDICAL CONDITIONS AND ATTRIBUTES

There are a few standard medical conditions that will cross a cannabis retail threshold on a daily basis. But what often is not considered are the behaviors that go hand-in-hand with the condition.

Getting to the root of the problem with patients can be quite a challenge. While some people cannot shut up about their medical issues, with others it is like pulling teeth. It is this latter type of patient who you must gently obtain certain information from if you are going to try to help them to the best of your ability. Knowing how to address not only the ailment, but the behaviors associated with them, will only make your job easier and more productive for both you and the patient.

CHRONIC PAIN

This is such a broad category that when someone responds that they are standing at your counter due to chronic pain, it really doesn't tell you anything at all. Is it from playing football in their high school glory days, or is it from recently diagnosed MS? Both of these examples come with their own behaviors. While the former jock is cranky from day in and day out pain for decades, the MS patient is frantic with fear from their new affliction in addition to the pain.

Chronic pain patients may walk with a cane or a limp or unbeknownst to them, physically favoring a certain part of their body.

- Paying attention to body language has a lot to do with your approach and recommendations. If you see them struggling to get across the room, offer them a chair at the counter.
- This will help to shift their attention from the pain to the conversation at hand.
- These patients can also be hard to please due to the fact they have tried every treatment under the sun, and nothing has worked.
- They find it hard to believe that cannabis will be any different. And even though their words may be cynical, the action that they took to be standing in front of you for help tells a different story.

Some can be extremely cranky, hard to please and can have an air of superiority about them.

- The superiority, I believe, comes from the daily battle against the pain and if they are standing in front of you, they have won the day. This is great, but they are alone in this accomplishment and therefore can seem a bit haughty.
- This is what it means to be pain-gry. Take the cranky with a grain of salt because you'd be crabby too if you were in constant pain.
- Think about the last time you were under the weather waiting in line at the drugstore for medicine that would make you feel better. You probably weren't the most personable person at the time.
- There also must be extra consideration if the patient is trying to kick painkillers, as withdrawal symptoms are definitely a factor.

When attempting to help those with chronic pain, asking the right questions is crucial. But it needs to be done in such a way that you are neither offensive nor pushy if you wish to have any success in helping them.

- Is their pain physical (muscle or nerve issues) or is it mental/emotional (stress or anxiety related) that is the root cause of the physical pain?

Let's say stress is keeping a patient up all night. They just can't seem to shut their head off long enough to fall asleep.

- This lack of rest causes tension headaches and achy muscles the next day from tossing and turning throughout the previous night.
- Even though a solid hybrid of cannabinoids and terpenes may help with the tensions of the day, a product heavy with myrcene or linalool can be useful for the evenings in trying to stop the awful cycle of not sleeping.
- Once the lack of proper rest is rectified, the daily hybrid will not be necessary.
- Always think in terms of preventative medicine. Cannabis is about taking less medication, not just more of a different kind of medicine.

ANXIETY

Back in my day we called them panic attacks. In doing research for a patient, I was almost offended to find that anxiety is considered an "emotion." The panic attacks I have known felt nothing short of 100% physical. I could hear my own heartbeat in my ears, I broke out in a cold sweat, and I always felt woozy on my own feet. Anyone who has experienced panic or anxiety attacks knows that they are all-encompassing, regardless of if their triggers are known.

Then there are those who are saddled with daily and uncontrollable anxiety, and the more you employ the following methods to your interactions, the better off the patient will be.

> Anxiety patients may speak extremely fast, ask continuous questions, or avoid eye contact to remove the attention from themselves as quickly as possible.

- Once you determine the needs of the patient, I have found it soothing to the patient if you just ramble on about a topic while you are putting their order together.
- This is a great opportunity to educate the patient while taking the focus off of them.
- Rapid-fire questioning may seem like accusatory behavior, but in fact is how some people handle their social situations.
- If the patient returns consistently, you'll find less and less of these behaviors as they begin to feel "safe" in your environment.

> When recommending cannabis to anxiety patients, it is very much a delicate balance. While some terpenes can double up on the paranoia, others mellow them out.

- Strong journaling by the individual and solid patient notes in your POS should cut down on the discovery period.
- Pay extra attention to which terpenes have been sampled by the patient, as some can actually make anxiety way worse.
- New-to-cannabis patients should always start with CBD and slowly add THC. This is assuming the patient isn't taking any drugs that will negatively interact.

> When anxiety patients have an "even" day (no waves of anxiety) they feel better about their condition and worry less in the evening, making it easier to fall asleep at night.

- A consultant should focus on finding the right product to reduce the daytime "waves."
- Once accomplished, there will be less of a need for the nighttime products.

> It is common for those with anxiety to suffer stomach issues due to the constant stress and worry.

- If available, CBG is showing promise for dealing with stomach issues and can be introduced with the same level of confidence as CBD, as it is also a nonintoxicating cannabinoid.

ADDICTION

Consulting a recovering addict can be a challenge, as there is no way of knowing where that person is in their recovery. It could have been less than 24 hours since their last fix, or they could be storing a 10-years-clean coin in their front left pocket. But regardless of their current milestone, they all must be treated with concern and respect, even if they are not returning the favor.

Addicts may lose focus or interest in the present moment.

- You may find that you must repeat yourself over and over and over again.

There may be several mood swings or behavioral changes, and the patient may become pushy or unfriendly for no reason.

- Try to adapt as seamlessly as possible and do not take it personally.
- Their "switch" may flick back and forth several times throughout the consultation.
- Of course, if the patient is totally out of line, you have to shut it down. You shouldn't be bullied just for trying to help someone who is struggling.

Distorted perception of reality can happen just as quickly as the mood swings.

- Information that was accepted at the beginning of the conversation can turn into a lie or a scam, in their mind.
- Ex: The $15 price tag on that pre-roll was a reasonable price to them until they are asked to pay for the product. "You said it was…" is not uncommon with these consults.

DEPRESSION

We have all felt a little down in the dumps from time to time. But for some, depression is a constant, crushing weight.

Consultants may have trouble with recommendations for these patients when "everything hurts." As general as this statement may be, there are answers in there, you just need to ask the right questions.

> **Some patients suffer depression by sleeping for days on end, while others spend days at a time staring at the idiot box.**

- Ask the patient if the symptoms of their depression seem more prevalent during the day or at night. This distinction will help guide you in your recommendations.
    - The constant slumbering patient may benefit from products with low levels of pinene or limoneme (uplifting) and CBD for its mood-altering potential.
    - This recommendation may help the patient to stave off naps during the day and therefore may help them to achieve a healthier sleep pattern.
    - But don't forget to remind them not to take these products too late in the day, as they may cause problems with falling asleep.
- The unmotivated, boob tube watching patient may benefit from products that have higher amount of the above mentioned pinene and limonene.
- These may get and keep this patient alert and moving around, which may promote feelings of accomplishment.
    - Statements such as "I know, I know" and "I doubt it will do any good" are very common during these discussions.
    - They are not being intentionally rude (most of the time), so it is better to gloss over these mini digs and jabs.
    - You may have to speed up your process by sharing a personal experience with the product to reassure them.
    - These patients may speak or move slowly, as if they are struggling with a great physical weight and have little regard for the conversation.

> **Patience is absolutely required—especially if you are busy—with these patients as any effort to rush them will only make them move slower.**

> **Please remember that these patients sometimes don't get much social interaction. In fact, this may be the only trip out of the house that day. Be kind.**

ALZHEIMER'S

Age-related conditions must be catered to, as this will be the majority of your patient demographic. But just because someone is of a certain age doesn't necessarily mean that they suffer from Alzheimer's. There are few common telltales to help you to confirm the affliction and then you can adjust your approach in a compassionate manner.

Alzheimer's patients can struggle with the simplest of common tasks as the disease progresses. Patients may struggle with or recount their money several times. Or it may take them several tries to open a door or answer when their name is called.

- Don't try to help with this (unless they really can't get it).
- They find it depressing, helpless and it just irritates them in general.
- Just be patient with them and offer a hand when warranted.
- These patients may be hesitant to pick up jars or magazines from counters on their own. If there is something you want them to check out, hand it to them.

They may get turned around in small spaces (losing the entrance/exit points) or simply wander away from your station and your conversation to roam around the room.

- In this case, come out from behind the counter and roam with them. Keep the conversation and the educating going. Adapt to the patient!

It's so easy to judge a person based on their appearance, especially if their grooming habits, clothing choices and hygiene are less than desirable.

- Just don't.
- Maybe this person has lost the ability to hold a toothbrush or a comb and haven't been able to admit it to themselves yet.
- We all have a battle going on!

PATIENT NOTES

I cannot stress the importance of solid patient notes in your POS enough. I encourage you to put in anything that you deem helpful. Maybe it's the name of a daughter who always comes in with Dad, or which branch of service the veteran was in, or how they are famous for trying to return half smoked joints (it's happened more than once).

So, even if it is only a few words, it really can help with giving everyone a heads-up on a patient's preferences, behaviors, and any potential compliance or product concerns, while making the patient feel taken care of.

PRODUCT COMPLAINTS

A product doesn't have to be on your shelf for very long for you to find out if a product is problematic. When presented with a complaint, regardless of your return policy, be apologetic and offer a remedy. Consultants also need to document any complaints for the following reasons.

CHRONIC COMPLAINERS

Some people you just can't please. Notes in the patient's file will give a consultant a heads-up on how it was handled in the past. You can use the same past remedy in hopes that if this person gets the same response every time, they may stop trying the same scam.

FAULTY PRODUCTS

It will be easier to take this issue up with the vendor if you have clear documentation showing a consistent problem with the product.

If a patient has complained about a product in the past and is attempting to buy it again, remind them that they didn't care for it the last time they bought it. People forget. Knowing at a glance what the patient has ordered in the past can help with future recommendations.

EXAMPLE

Dan states that he has been unhappy with his last couple of flower purchases. His patient notes indicate that he has bought heavy sativas both times and is about to buy another one.

By paying attention in this manner a budtender can recommend something more along the lines of a hybrid in hopes that Dan will be satisfied with his next purchase.

EXAMPLE

Dolly wants her quarter ounce packaged in individual grams. To me this screams "resale." I would just tell her that it is against shop policy to break up a quarter ounce into separate packages due to the possibility of resale.

If Dolly is elderly and needs help with measuring out her dosages, you can always show her what one gram will look like and she can split it up herself.

POS NOTES

Notes on any potential compliance issues help document and decipher if there really is something fishy going on.

These notes are another means of communication between budtenders who have helped the same patient.

EXAMPLES

Jack takes his time and wanders around the room. According to his notes following him around the room will speed up his tire-kicking time.

Jane complains at every visit about the prices and always tries to get freebies. A gentle reminder of which days have which specials quiets her demands.

REMEDIES FOR HARASSMENT AND DIFFICULT CUSTOMERS

It requires very thick skin to work in cannabis retail. I had a managing partner once ask what I mean by that. I told him that some people find that they simply do not have the stomach for it. It's a different beast of retail. Dealing with people's medical conditions and complaints can be extremely challenging day in and day out.

I have been called so many names over the years while standing behind the cannabis counter that I've lost count. But two really stick out and still make me chuckle to this day. The first one is when a woman called me a "bad apple" (hehe), because I wouldn't let her return a half-eaten edible. My other favorite is when a voluptuous family of five all wanted to come into the med room together. We had very limited space and our policy called for no more than two at a time. I told them I would make an exception, and they could go back in two groups (one of two and the other of three). Unsatisfied with my efforts, I was called a "snarky bitch." I actually laughed at this guy and said, "Now I am retracting my compromise to our store policy. We only allow two back at a time." And I walked away.

BULLIES

Bullying is a big problem in the cannabis industry. It's disgraceful that bullying has become so commonplace in cannabis that it is tolerated, and sometimes even accommodated. The same sensible edict that is granted to pharmacies, gas stations, and grocery stores, is simply not being enforced in cannabis retail.

Some cheeky patients are delusional, thinking that because they spend a certain number of dollars at your store, know somebody in the business, or because they bring a friend with them that they deserve recognition in the form of a kickback.

STOP BULLYING

I don't know about you, but I drop some serious coin at the grocery store and at the gas stations every week. Yet, if I was to approach the gas station attendant, and demand that I deserve a free tank of gas because of the money I spend there, I would be laughed out of the place. And what do you think would happen if I walked up to the cashier at the grocery store and announced that I had brought my friend along, and followed it up with, "What do I get for doing that?" And heaven knows that I certainly didn't get extra pills in my prescriptions because I knew the pharmacist by name.

So, where did this notion that dispensaries work on the level as backroad flea markets come from?

Does it stem from past interactions with the black market? I highly doubt it. The fact is you didn't dicker about the price of the product with your supplier in the parking lot of the local pizza joint.

Is there a sense of entitlement by association? Bullies are famous for name-dropping, in the hopes that the budtender is either impressed or cowed by the possibility that they are "friends" with the owner or vendors in the local industry. Try again. Everyone knows "a guy." If they are so in tune with the pulse of the cannabis industry, they wouldn't be standing at a dispensary counter, giving the budtender a hard time, asking for free product.

Could it possibly be an age thing? The majority of cannabis retail employees are in their 20s, while the middle of the road for cannabis patients is their late 40s. So, do these harassing patients feel they are superior to the younger generation behind the counter? Does their advanced age warrant them that free pre-roll, and no young punk is going to deny them these self-proclaimed rights? Or is it simply because they have endured the struggle of buying their medication underground for so long? Please, not that old chestnut.

When denied, the classic five-year-old playground bully reaction will lead them to spending the rest of their consultation passively throwing little digs about the lack of quality product being offered. This is mixed in with attempts to belittle the budtender with their "expertise" in all thing's cannabis (which is usually just more bullshit and bravado). I have even observed them huffing and grumbling and shuffling their feet in a restrained form of a temper tantrum while browsing the displays. Yes, these are fully grown men and women acting this way.

Bullies can smell fear. Aggressors will take any opening to browbeat a timid employee with loud declarations of how much money they spend weekly, that they even bring friends with them to make your store more money, and how XYZ store accommodates their demands. This intimidates and wears down an unprepared budtender. It muddles their perspective of who is really calling the shots.

As this forced professional fatigue shows signs of taking its toll, this predator instinctively knows that their odds are inching them toward getting what they want.

Now they lay the beratement on even thicker, pushing the counter person to turn to management to ask if they can throw in something extra. If management concedes, even if they only do so to get this unruly patient to leave the store, the bully has won. This combative victory will be twisted into "the budtender did it for me last time" in the future, and then they will proceed to run with it until the wheels fall off.

Bullies have always been a part of the retail consumer demographic and are not likely to fade away anytime soon. Therefore, proper budtender training on how to diffuse these bullies and retain a strict store policy is essential. You have to stop feeding these monsters. This is your house, own it.

So, regardless of their justifications, how is a budtender to professionally defend themselves against this increasingly popular type of harassment?

The most common reaction, and the right one, is the "shut down." The following calm, canned responses will give you an idea on how to shut them down, and how you can tweak your own premeditated responses.

HARASSMENT EXAMPLES

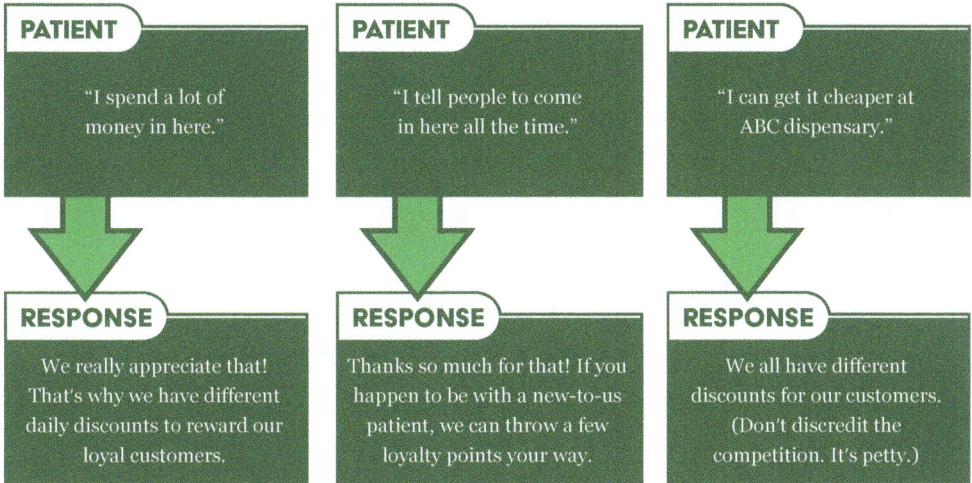

PATIENT

"I spend a lot of money in here."

PATIENT

"I tell people to come in here all the time."

PATIENT

"I can get it cheaper at ABC dispensary."

RESPONSE

We really appreciate that! That's why we have different daily discounts to reward our loyal customers.

RESPONSE

Thanks so much for that! If you happen to be with a new-to-us patient, we can throw a few loyalty points your way.

RESPONSE

We all have different discounts for our customers. (Don't discredit the competition. It's petty.)

Between your referral programs, senior, veteran, and daily promotions, there is something for everyone.

If a problematic customer still cannot be calmed or deterred by some variation of the above remedies, it is up to management (when given authority) to properly shut it down. Some of the locations I have worked for used the three-strike approach, some wanted the decision to go through the higher-ups, and others just left these decisions to the floor manager. I have always tried to give these types of people multiple opportunities to keep themselves off of the banned list. I've made notes in patient files to ensure that maybe a specific budtender should not be assisting a specific customer. I have stuck my nose in conversations that smell of conflict to try to neutralize the situation, and I have even asked, "You like coming here, don't you? You would like to continue to, wouldn't you?" If these didn't work and the customer was still aggressive, I would make sure that they understood what the consequences would be.

I was plugging away at my managerial mountain of emails in my office when Penny knocked on my door to tell me that she was fed up with the customer she was trying to help. She explained that the guy kept taking age-related jabs at her and was combative to the point of taking products out of his basket and tossing them back behind the counter like he was sifting through a recycling bin. She finally told him that she had to run in the back to do a price check just to regain her patience and let me know what was up. Penny was a solid employee who could always handle whatever situation arose. So, the fact that she was in my doorway and at a loss with this guy spoke volumes.

Setting my correspondence aside, I followed her back out onto the floor to assess the situation for myself by straightening a shelf within earshot. She had barely bellied back up to her station when the guy said, "Needed someone to do the math for you, didn't you? I'm not surprised. None of you kids know how to count without your fingers."

Penny cooly responded with, "Not at all. I was checking to see if yesterday's flower discount still applied. It doesn't." This guy took this as free passage to continue to berate my budtender. "Why would you try to sell me any then? You're a special kind of stupid, aren't you?" That was all I needed to hear.

I walked up next to Penny, took this guy's basket filled with his selections, and put it under the counter. "You're done. We are not here for you to beat up just because you are having a bad day and need someone to take it out on. We are only here to help. I will not have anyone treating my employees the way I heard you just treating Penny here." With eyes as wide as saucers, he began to sputter and whine that she wasn't doing this, and she wasn't doing that. Grabbing his name with a glance at the screen, I continued with, "Mr. Otto you are no longer welcome here. You are banned. There's the door. Use it." Like an overgrown spoiled brat in the grocery store, he began to yell, "This place sucks! Everything here is trash! You all are just so ... so ... useless!" as he stormed out the door. I told Penny to put detailed notes in his profile about the interaction and add "banned" in red capital letters at the top with my initials for authorization.

Some days later, Penny gave me the nod toward the lobby as Mr. Otto was trying to check in. This ought to be good, I thought as I headed for the door. I directed the guy into the corner of the lobby just in case he wanted to cause a scene again. "What part of banned didn't you understand? Are you going to start ranting and raving again at our customers Mr. Otto? Because if you are, I have no problem calling the police," I said, crossing my arms over my chest. Mr. Otto put his hands up in a defensive position as he explained that he was in fact having a bad day the last time. And that he was so very sorry, and if I could give him another chance, he'd never do it again. I wasn't completely convinced that this guy even realized what he had done wrong to earn himself the banishment in the first place.

So, I thought to get creative. "I tell you what. The budtender that you used as a verbal punching bag the last time just happens to be working today. I will leave this decision up to her. I'll let her know that you would like to speak with her. She may come out, she may not. You can plead your case with her and if she is in a forgiving mood, I will lift the ban. If she isn't, and I wouldn't blame her, the ban stays."

So that is exactly what I did. I gave Penny the lowdown on how I wanted to handle this situation and that I was good with whatever she decided. I also recommended that she made the guy sweat it out for at least 20 minutes if she did decide to hear him out. No point in giving priority to people like that, I thought as I returned to my desk. I never saw how much time Penny spent in the lobby, but I did check Mr. Otto's profile at the end of the day which read "ban lifted" in green with the date and my initials.

BOSS BULLIES

Bully status isn't just reserved for customers. There is a large bullying problem with the owners of some of these cannabis companies as well. You will find crazy turnover numbers in the cannabis space, because when you treat someone like they are disposable, this is exactly how they will act. Some of the bosses I have known over the years have been scam artists, dirtbags, cowards, and narcissists of biblical proportions.

Working for owners who have never run a staff or have never had employees of their own is quite problematic. They have no clue on how to juggle single moms, young adults in college, or interact with the human condition. They do not see their employees as human, but as property. In fact, the majority of issues that I have had in the cannabis retail space stem from the higher-ups treating their employees like cattle.

These examples of crappy human behavior have ranged from owners threatening termination if employees were found to be socializing after hours, to being banned from having any contact at all with someone who was a former employee. As if they owned these people's lives completely.

I have witnessed a newly pregnant mother go from 30 hours a week to 5 hours once the owners were notified of her condition. They have scheduled single moms with little ones to work on Halloween night and Christmas Eve (even when they weren't normal scheduled days), while giving their family members two weeks off for the holiday. Paid. I have applauded CEOs for hiring the handicapped only to find that months later they had forced this person to complete a task that they were clearly physically incapable of carrying out. When I pushed back, their response was, "If they can't do it, they can't work here."

People have quietly resigned just to have the owners hold their last paycheck until the former employees had to retain an attorney to get what was owed.

I have witnessed an owner just hours away from shutting down the business without so much as a heads-up to their employees (mostly single parents and college kids). The response was, "They'll find out when they show up for work tomorrow."

I have stated very clearly to every single cannabis company I have worked for, subcontracted or not, that I will remain loyal and work tirelessly (in some cases pulling close to 80 hours a week) as long as they are not hurting anyone. Simple enough, right?

But unfortunately, more times than not, once these owners began to make a couple of bucks, they lost sight of the mantra that had me wanting to work for them in the first place. "Patients over Profits" T-shirts were worn while the staff was forced to remove expiration dates from products and parading a physically disabled child in advertisements to bring traffic in the door. As the old saying goes, a financial windfall will make good people better and bad people worse.

So, for those of you who like to pass judgment on employment turnover or those who think they have me pegged because I have worked for several different cannabis companies over the years, know that the above examples are only the "reader friendly" ones. I still stand by my reasons for moving on. I absolutely refuse to work for garbage human beings.

FIRST CONSULT WITH NEW-TO-CANNABIS CONSUMERS

Employees must recognize that they have a responsibility to the consumer to offer educated information. If you find yourself unsure, it is always better to say that you don't know than give false information. You must master the art of "I don't know." When done correctly you are showing the consumer that although you do not have the answer, you do care for their plight and will find them a solution. Employees should also never, ever use the "C" word. No, not that one, but the word "cure." There simply isn't enough research to support this claim, and the last thing you want to do is give someone false hope. But what we can say is that cannabis has the potential to help with the right conditions. When speaking about what cannabis may do for someone, I have always found it best to stick with the following phrases.

RECOMMENDATIONS & RESPONSIBILITY

EMPLOYEES SHOULD USE PHRASES SUCH AS:

"I have personally found..."

"Current research suggests..."
(Cite credible references)

"Patients have reported..."

The first few questions you ask new-to-cannabis consumers are critical if you are going to help this person to the best of your ability.

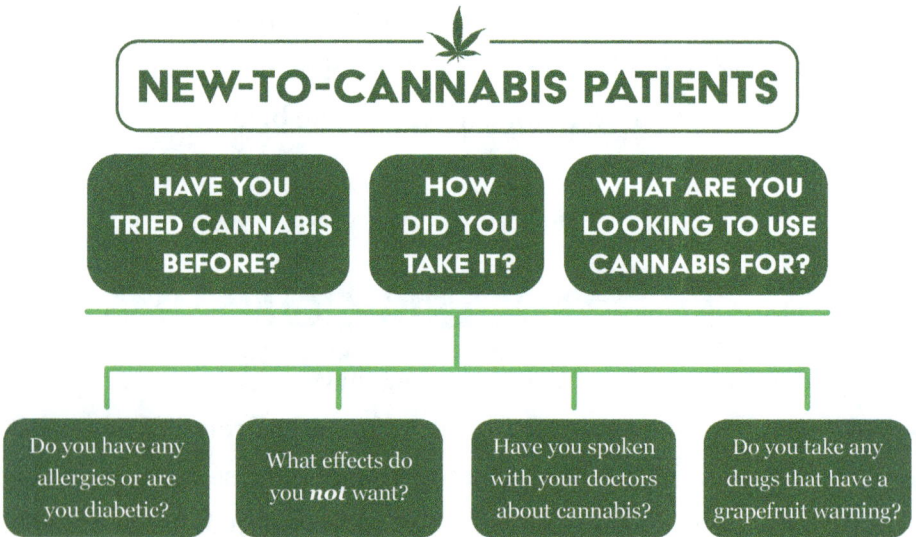

NEW-TO-CANNABIS PATIENTS

HAVE YOU TRIED CANNABIS BEFORE?

HOW DID YOU TAKE IT?

WHAT ARE YOU LOOKING TO USE CANNABIS FOR?

Do you have any allergies or are you diabetic?

What effects do you *not* want?

Have you spoken with your doctors about cannabis?

Do you take any drugs that have a grapefruit warning?

I learned the weight-of-my-words lesson the hard way. I was speaking to a group at a local American House on the very basics of using cannabis as medicine. This included a bit on how CBD can be compared to an anti-inflammatory like Advil or Motrin, but should not be purchased from gas stations, but state licensed facilities after getting permission from their doctors. After my presentation I packed up and made my way back to the shop. Before I had even made it a mile down the road, I had the director of the facility calling me to say there was an irate family member wanting to speak with me. I racked my brain on the way back to the facility about what I could've possibly have said to get a family member all wound up!

It turned out that the very, very angry gentleman's mother was in attendance for my presentation and took my information about CBD to mean quite literally that she could stop taking all of her pills if she could just get a ride to the gas station. Dementia is a jerk. No wonder this guy was livid. Both the director and I gushed apologies and explained what was actually said, and that it was his mother who had gotten it twisted around. Of course, this didn't matter to the son as we could all hear his mother continuing to holler from the second floor about a ride to the gas station.

It just goes to show that you can say and do all of the right things and stupid shit can still happen.

LEGENDS, HALF-TRUTHS, AND NONSENSE

With the constant swirl of pot politics and celebrity endorsements, some truly amazing pioneers are not getting the limelight I believe they deserve. I will try to do them some justice in the following section, which also includes how misinformation in the cannabis industry isn't only reserved for the effects that it can have on the human condition. There are a ton of urban legends that have been created by the storyteller stoners over the decades. Some have merit, some were based on a truth at some point, and others are just complete hogwash.

420

Oh, the wonder of our beloved holiday! Live music, food trucks, bundle deals, and freebies as far as our red eyes can see. Retailers spend months planning for the 20th day of April and for good reason. 420 is often explained as the St. Paddy's Day for stoners (minus the car bomb shots and vomit), and brings in crowds from far and wide. The last time I worked retail on a 420, it was a slushy, nasty Michigan day, yet we still saw over 500 people. Many a midnight toker has spent their day bouncing around to the different dispensaries to collect as much free stuff as they possibly can. These goodies can range from bud to Bic lighters and bandanas with purchase of course.

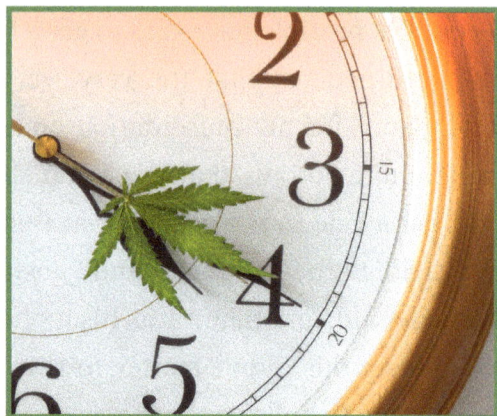

In preparation for the circus ahead of us, I had asked my staff that morning to retell the story of how the holiday got its roots, as the question would be asked over and over again throughout the day. I have to say that I was a bit disappointed to find that not one of the dozen stoners in front of me really knew, so I gathered them around for the details behind the folklore.

It is easy to get this story wrong, as there are many variations and urban legends surrounding the date and its meaning. Some believe that it is the number of active chemicals in Marijuana (NIH states 540)[83], some reference it to Hitler's birthday (in 1889), and others credit Bob Dylan and his tune "Rainy Day Woman No. 12 & 35" for the lyrics "everybody must get stoned," because 12 multiplied by 35 does, in fact equal 420.[84] And if you are a baseball fan, you should know that both Fenway Park and Tiger Stadium both opened on April 20th, 1912.[85]

But the reality is that the roots of the 420 legend can be traced back to five teenage athletes who attended San Rafael High School in California. In true stoner simplicity, they coined themselves "The Waldos" from the wall they would hang out on campus. They had caught wind in the fall of 1971 that a member of the Coast Guard had planted a crop of unattended weed in the area, and it was even said that there was a "treasure" map drawn by the coastie himself. So, the quintet began meeting at the Louis Pasteur statue outside of the school at 4:20 p.m. at least once a week in search of the field of green. They never did find the unsecured crop, but the term 420 stuck around, as a way for teens to reference pot without the adults being any the wiser.[86]

710

July 10th (7/10) is a fairly new holiday in the stoner culture. It comes with most of the fanfare that 420 does, but it does cater to a younger crowd. It is a day to celebrate and partake in concentrates, aka oil. If you take the word "OIL" and turn it upside down, you get "710." That's it. That's the whole story. It's not rocket science folks, and I feel like there should be a blonde joke in there somewhere.

JACK HERER (JUNE 18, 1939 – APRIL 15, 2010)

When one speaks of true cannabis activism and the fight for legalization, Jack Herer should be on the top of the list. He has been called the "Emperor of Hemp" and the "Godfather of the cannabis movement" and even has a very popular cannabis strain named after him. In 1985 he wrote the now classic *The Emperor Wears No Clothes*, which has been used to motivate and inspire those looking to continue to fight for hemp derived medicine, food, and fiber.[87]

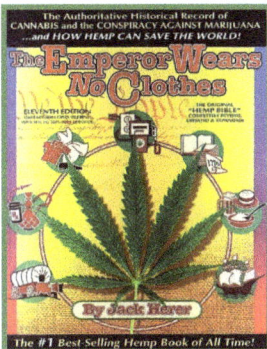

What Jack had started is still celebrated with the competition of The Jack Herer Cup held each year in Columbia, Amsterdam, Las Vegas, and Oklahoma City.[88]

My favorite quote from the man is, "Hemp will be the future of all mankind, or there won't be a future." I don't think he's wrong.

HOTBOXING

If you have ever seen the cult classic *Fast Times at Ridgemont High*, you will remember the scene where all the guys pile out of the van in a cloud of smoke. This is known as hotboxing. It is the act of confining yourself in a space that exposes you to a heavy amount of secondhand cannabis smoke. There are many who are afraid of getting a "contact high," or popping positive on a drug test just from being around this smoke. So, can someone catch a buzz just by being in the same room as someone smoking a joint?

"Researchers measured the amount of THC in the blood of people who do not smoke marijuana and had spent 3 hours in a well-ventilated space with people casually smoking marijuana; THC was present in the blood of the nonsmoking participants, but the amount was well below the level needed to fail a drug test. Another study that varied the levels of ventilation and the potency of the marijuana found that some nonsmoking participants exposed for an hour to high-THC marijuana (11.3% THC concentration) in an unventilated room showed positive urine assays in the hours directly following exposure; a follow-up study showed that nonsmoking people in a confined space with people smoking high-THC marijuana reported mild subjective effects of the drug—a 'contact high'—and displayed mild impairments on performance in motor tasks."[89]

If you are concerned with having THC in your system, small amounts or not, I suggest that you remove yourself from the space. Better safe than sorry.

RICK SIMPSON

Just about everyone into cannabis for medical reasons has heard of RSO (aka Rick Simpson Oil). If you haven't, it's a highly concentrated, dark, sticky, diabolical-looking product usually packaged in syringes or capsules.

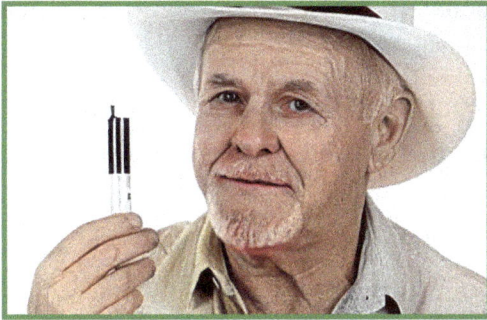

Rick Simpson was an engineer from Canada who had suffered a head injury in 1997, and due to the side effects of his prescribed pills, he went looking for an alternative solution. He began using extractions from the cannabis he grew in his own backyard, and it seemed to do the trick. So, he took it upon himself to share his story, give away the concoction (and recipe) for free, and became an activist for legal access to medical marijuana.[90]

In 2003 Rick was diagnosed with a common skin cancer and thought to use the same tar-like substance topically to see if it would help. He claims that it cleared up his cancer in just four days, and though recent research does not necessarily support the short time frame, it is showing promise as a treatment for skin cancer.

Because people can be just the absolute worst, there are plenty of fake RSO sites out there riding on the coattails of Mr. Simpson. According to his original site, Phoenix Tears, he is only affiliated with www.simpsonramadur.com and www. phoenixtears.ca

HENRY FORD'S HEMP CAR

Funny how a girl who was born and raised in the Motor City, where just about everyone's employment was tied to the automotive industry in some fashion, had to extend her reach all the way south of the Mason-Dixon Line to get the truth about a car.

Now, I have seen plenty of publications and documentaries on Henry Ford's famous "hemp car" over the years, but when gathering information on the subject I had found that none of them seemed to match. So, I reached out to the distinguished author of *Tales from the Kentucky Hemp Highway*, Dan Isenstein, for some clarification from a true hemp historian.

Dan has been gracious enough to contribute the following summary on the subject, and if the history of hemp's use in the US sparks your interest, be sure to check out his book!

HENRY FORD'S HEMP CAR THAT WASN'T

There is a popular legend that in the 1930s Henry Ford grew hemp so he could make a car out of hemp that ran on hemp fuel. Thanks to the internet, this is a widely circulated story, but how much of this legend is true and how much is just hempsters blowing smoke?

Interest in exploring nonfood uses for crops started to gain favor in the years following the First World War, and reached its peak during the Great Depression, especially in the years just preceding the United States' entry into the Second World War. The advocates of this new avenue of scientific investigation believed that through chemistry, America's agricultural bounty could be converted into the raw materials for countless products from fuel to plastics.

The promise of converting agricultural produce into alternative fuels and raw materials for manufacturing caught the attention of Henry Ford. Ford's interest in the potential of chemistry and the farm to supply the materials required to manufacture and power automobiles helped to provide scientists with a great deal of credibility. This interest culminated in the production of a prototype vehicle, and legend has it this car was made from and powered by hemp.

While many toiled developing "nonfood uses for crops," the new field of science was not named "chemurgy" until 1934 when William J. Hale, an important figurehead of the Dow Chemical Corporation, wrote the highly influential book *The Farm Chemurgic*.

Ford saw potential in the chemurgic movement and on May 7, 1935, the first National Chemurgic conference was held at his research lab in Dearborn.

The conference identified developing a fuel-alcohol product, "Agrol," as the top priority for the council. Initially conceived and proposed as a gasoline additive, Agrol was developed to eliminate knocks and increase octane. However, the leadership of the National Farm Chemurgic, namely Garvan and Hale, were outspoken in their almost religious belief that fuel-alcohol could eventually replace gasoline altogether in internal combustion engines.

The obstacles facing the development of fuel-alcohol were substantial. The sometimes antagonistic and outlandish statements made by some of the council's leaders made them worse. A project of such scope required partners both in government and the private sector. But, both Francis Garvan of the Chemical Foundation and Hale had made powerful enemies; Garvan vocally targeted the petroleum industry, while Hale was an outspoken critic of the US Department of Agriculture.

While the fuel alcohol project was the council's focus, research into alternative manufacturing materials was the second priority. Ford was personally interested in finding new materials that could replace imported raw materials like rubber and expensive domestically produced materials like steel.

In 1941, just prior to World War II, Ford's in-house team completed a prototype vehicle. The car was built on a tubular steel frame and incorporated phenolic resin body panels embedded with natural fibers, which included among other things hemp, flax, and kenaf. It was designed to run on Agrol. A second prototype under construction at the outbreak of the Second World War was scrapped as Ford and the rest of the nation dedicated its manufacturing capacity to the war effort. Likewise, all chemurgic research was now devoted to supporting the war effort. The first prototype was also destroyed.

The manufacturing process used to make plastic body panels for Ford's prototype was time consuming and would have been inefficient for large scale production. The narrative that there was significant hemp content in Ford's chemurgic car is simply not true. Hemp comprised an extremely small proportion of the prototype vehicle produced.

The premise that "anything made from plastic can be made of hemp," is essentially meme bait simply paraphrasing a concept Hale considered core to "chemurgy," that anything made from a "hydrocarbon" (petroleum) could be made from a "carbohydrate" (plant matter). Research into developing industrial raw materials from organic material or agricultural products continues to this day. No longer called "chemurgy," this field of research is now called "biomechanical engineering."

If there were truly more to the story of Henry Ford's "hemp plastic car that runs on hemp fuel," it would be more than a meme. The idea of a "hemp" car or a "hemp" airplane inspires the imagination, but the reality of hemp-based manufacturing materials is that they were and currently remain a novelty.[91]

RICHARD ROSE

I have been a fan of Richard Rose since the beginning of my career in cannabis. Initially, it wasn't for his hardcore entrepreneurship or the historical changes that he impressed upon our food industry (which I was ignorant of until now), but his humanity. His honest sincerity to help his fellow humans.

Forty years ago, Richard started an entire crusade, which became hemp's first billion-dollar industry, by being the first to bring smart-branded foods made from hemp seed to the masses. Coined the "Tofu Mogul," and rightfully so, having also been the first to offer such products as vegan eggnog (1981), tofu frozen dessert powdered mixes (1985), tofu ice cream exported to Japan (1986), organic vegan cream cheese (1994), and all while running the first vegan restaurant in California in 1980.[92] Whew!

As if he didn't have enough going on, Richard decided to shift his focus to hemp in 1994. Hemp was a better source of protein and had been around long enough to support this claim. So, why not replace the soy in our food industry with shelled hemp seeds? And since nobody was importing non-sterilized hemp seeds at the time, he put his million dollar businesses and his freedom on the line to introduce shelled hempseed to North America.

This accomplishment earned him another title as "The Hemp Nut," named after his company HempNut Inc., which from 1994–2002 was groundbreaking for creating the best practices for hemp seed foods in North America. Richard's products were so on point that his "Hempeh Burger" had an FDA health claim that it actually reduced the risk of heart disease.[93] That commendation didn't just fall in his lap, he earned it.

In true Mr. Rose style, he continued to cross the finish line first with hemp food sold in a military PX (1996), introducing shelled hempseed to the US and Canada (1996), and organizing a 27-member international supply chain to export hemp seed to Europe, Canada, Japan, China, and Australia.[94]

Then, as if Richard wasn't doing enough to help the health of his fellow humans, he added CBD to his revolutionary resume. He created "Nobacco" and "Not-Pot," which are made out of craft hemp flower that can be smoked. He started the Medicinal Hemp Association, the Hemp Flower

Products Association, and even brought the Hemp Food Association back from the grave.

Even with decades of noble accomplishments, my favorite thing about Mr. Rose is that he is always willing to teach, always willing to share his knowledge and ideas regardless of where you are on the totem pole of life. To this end, he has created a free cannabis library (CannLib) with over twenty thousand PDFs relating to cannabis and offers "CannaSearch," which grants access to the cannabis research of 64 different medical conditions so people can learn for themselves.[95]

Of course, anyone who has been in the cannabis industry for long enough cannot help but to have a sense of humor, and Richard is no different. When asked during an interview with *Hemp Today* if they could call him a "guru," Richard responded with, "I've been called far worse by those engaged in f***ery of the first order. But if you insist, call me "CannGuru" ... I have all kinds of ideas in my pouch."[96] I'm willing to bet the hemp farm that he does.

"MANGOES INCREASE YOUR HIGH."

Most of us have heard this one. It is the theory that if you combine mangos with your cannabis intake you will get higher because you are doubling down on the terpene myrcene. Although that mango smoothie you have is extra yummy and does a fine job at squashing your cottonmouth, it isn't enhancing your buzz. Contrary to popular belief, mangos really don't contain high concentrations of myrcene, and what myrcene it does have is not housed in the

fleshy fruit, but in the skin. And if you were thinking about eating just the skin of a mango, I'd listen to the following warning by Dr. Codi Peterson, "... mangoes contain urushiol, the same compound present in poison ivy and poison oak. So don't start eating mango skins to get extra high or you're likely to bite off more than you bargained for."[97]

"HOLDING YOUR HIT GETS YOU HIGHER."

There is a fairy tale that the longer you hold your toke the higher you will get. I'm here to tell you that all of your eye-watering, red-faced choking is for naught.

How high you get from smoking cannabis has more to do with THC potency than the actual time spent holding your breath. This is because when THC is inhaled, it heads straight to the alveoli (air sacs in the lungs), and any available cannabinoids will be absorbed within mere seconds and then pushed in the direction of your bloodstream. Holding your breath past this point is only holding on to the harmful byproducts and carcinogens of smoking.[98] Stop it.

A STONER LOVE STORY

I couldn't say what day of the week it was, but I do remember the vibe in the room. We were all beat up from the feet up by patients and technology pushing us around all day. We had endured everything from the ATM spitting out fives instead of twenties (the keys were M.I.A.), to a woman ranting that the topical we sold her gave her diarrhea, and when asked if she actually ate the topical, she responded with smashing a tip jar on the floor before stomping out. Mama said there would be days like this.

I had just sent our receptionist for a much needed break after another relentless rush, and the closest budtender gladly took her place simply for the opportunity to sit and rest her barking dogs. With everyone on the floor doing some sort of recouping, I took the next patient to give them some additional time.

My customer service tank was running on fumes, but I still managed a "Hi darling. What brings you in?" The tall, Dean Martin–look-alike before me answered that he was hurting from building a firepit all day and could use a few pre-rolls for the pain.

I turned toward the shelves that held the glass jars filled with our offerings when he added with a voice like a bass drum, "got anything that won't make me cough?" Speaking over my shoulder, I matched his question with one of my own.

"Are you holding in your hit?"

"Well, yeah. That's how we were taught to do it in middle school," he answered with dimples tugging at the corners of his smile.

Handsome or not, I was in no mood for playful banter and snapped back with, "Stop listening to 7th graders. The only thing you are holding in are the carcinogens from the smoke. Any of the good stuff gets into your lungs much faster than you would think. Plus holding your breath, even without smoke in your lungs, will get you lightheaded. So, if your argument is that it gets you higher, try again."

I didn't give him the opportunity to reply, and I moved the interaction along by picking out two pre-rolls that were a bit smoother than the others. As I went to ring him up, he informed me that his bank card wasn't working and sheepishly handed me a double, large-handed fistful of quarters. And why not? This was how the whole day had been. But I honestly didn't care at this point. It wasn't my money after all, as long as it added up. With a Lili Von Shtupp "I'm so tired" smile, I sent him on his way.

A few days later he came back to let me know that he did try my advice on how to properly smoke a joint and that he did indeed cough less. Requesting a few more of the same pre-rolls that he purchased earlier that week, he not only relayed that he had "folding money" this time but would like to hang out and scribbled his number on a flyer on the counter.

Maybe it was the boyish dimpled grin, or his gravelly voice, or maybe it was because he could actually build things with his own two hands (honestly, who does that anymore), that got my attention.

I no longer question the fates about how I was found by my knight in shining armor in a pot shop, surly as hell. Because regardless, to this very day I am so thankful that he was still using middle school ministry and that my brand of snark didn't deter him. He has been making me sway for years now, and after suffering through a few of my "respect the herb" speeches and getting him to ditch the homemade pop can pipes, I am still absolutely smitten with the man that is the love of my life.

WAKE AND BAKE

If you don't know the term, it is when you smoke cannabis first thing when you wake up. If you smoke with your morning cuppa Joe, it is called a "hippie speedball."

Partaking within the first hour of waking up is more popular than one might think.

A global drug survey from 2017 shows that Americans have the highest rate of any country at 21.9%. Mexico is next in line at 18.4%, Greece is at 15.9%, our brother to the north comes in at 14.9%, and lastly Brazil at 14.3%.[99]

People report that when doing this they feel "higher," and for a longer period of time than if they were to consume later in the day. Some guess that the reason is because you are still sleepy or that your body hasn't moved around any nutrients during your slumber. But a more scientific approach to the question might be closer to the truth.

At this point you know that our ECS is a regulator. This also includes our circadian rhythm (our internal clock that tells us when we are hungry and when to fall asleep and wake up).

According to an article scientifically reviewed by Codi Peterson, PharmD, "Research has shown that the amounts of all three components of the ECS, endocannabinoids, receptors, and enzymes fluctuate throughout the day. One study of healthy adults found that the levels of anandamide, one of the two

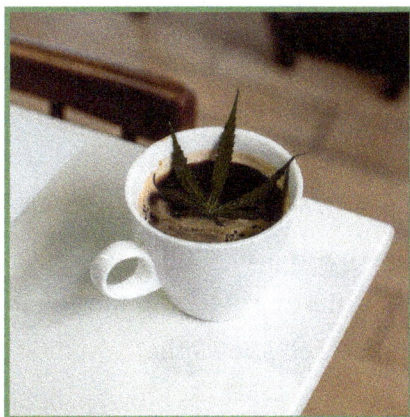

major endocannabinoids, are three times higher after waking up compared to immediately before sleep."[100]

But whatever the reason, there are things to consider before choosing to wake and bake. What do you have planned for the day? Will you be driving any time soon? These answers will tell you if you have the luxury of a slow sipping hippie speedball for breakfast.

"WHITE ASH MEANS IT'S CLEAN."

This one has been hanging around for decades, and you will still find inconclusive arguments on the topic. The idea is that if the ashes at the end of your joint or in your bowl are white, you have a high quality, clean flower you are smoking on.

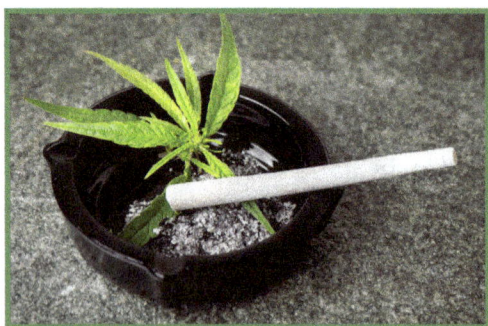

To find black ashes at the end means you're smoking garbage that may be filled with chemicals or wasn't harvested properly.

One opinion will say that the black or dark gray ash comes from the plant not being "flushed" prior to harvest. "Flushing" is when a grower will only offer the plant clean water in the last few weeks before harvesting to flush out any extra nutrients or fertilizers from the soils that the plant has been feeding on.

Another opinion is that the flowers from the plant were not cured (dried) properly, and it is the excess moisture that is to blame for the dark ashes. Much like wood on a campfire, when dry wood is involved, you will get white or light gray ashes at the base of your firepit. But if you were to try to burn wet wood, you end up with coal-like chunks that never fully break down into ashes.

And then there is the role that combustion plays in smoking cannabis. "Research shows that when combustion takes place at a high temperature, organic material is burnt properly leading to a low concentration of nitrogen, and by extension, clear ash colors. On the other hand, when combustion occurs at a low temperature, organic compounds are not properly burnt, thereby leaving a darker ash color."[101]

So, this tells us that the ash color may have everything to do with the temperatures of combustion and not the quality of our flower.

"WEED HASN'T KILLED ANYONE, SO IT'S TOTALLY SAFE."

Ummmm .... no.

This assumption is reckless. To also say that cannabis is a plant, so therefore it is harmless, is another stupid statement.

Cocaine comes from a plant. Heroin comes from a plant. Your argument is invalid.

Let's say you took a healthy, middle-aged person with zero medical conditions and they took zero medications; the statement that "no one has died from cannabis," would be true. But realistically, who can check all of those boxes? Just about everyone has something or takes something (including supplements). This opens doors for potential interactions and/or adverse effects which could have grave results. Plus, if you are not growing it yourself there is always the chance that some idiot has used toxic growing practices or has sprayed something ungodly on their products.

But in the grand scheme of things of what people can take for either medicinal or recreational purposes, clean cannabis is way, way, way safer than prescriptions, alcohol, or other drugs.

PURPLE FLOWER

All right folks, that is quite enough. Stop drinking the purple Kool-Aid! Just because a bud is purple does not mean that it is extra strong or special.

If you are attempting to grow "purps," know that the flower has to have a genetic predisposition for a high concentration of anthocyanins (a group of flavonoids responsible for the colors in fruits and veggies) and it is the environment that coaxes out the color. When your plant is exposed to colder temperatures, the chlorophyll begins to break down and makes room for the color-producing anthocyanins. This is also how we get our amazing fall colors.[102]

So why are people drawn to the purple nugs in display jars? Because they look different—exotic if you will—and those marketing cannabis flower know the general public are suckers for cool packaging (guilty). So, if you insist on using your eyes instead of your nose as your go-to method in choosing a flower, just look for the frosty goodness of the trichomes.

HASH BASH – JOHN SINCLAIR

The history of the Ann Arbor Hash Bash begins with John Sinclair's possession of two (yes, just two) joints which landed him a ten-year prison sentence in 1969 under Michigan's felony marijuana laws. The December 10, 1971, "John Sinclair Freedom Rally" at Crisler Center arena brought together John Lennon, Yoko Ono, Stevie Wonder, and Bob Seger, among others, to join Sinclair's wife, Leni, in pushing for his release. Sinclair had been in prison for over two years at this point. Lennon even wrote a new song for the occasion, "John Sinclair."

On March 9th, 1972, the Michigan Supreme Court decided that the laws used to convict John Sinclair were unconstitutional, and Michigan legislature changed marijuana possession into a misdemeanor. With a small window of opportunity, as this new classification didn't kick in until April 3rd, the still-anonymous founders suggested they throw a "hash festival" on April Fool's Day to celebrate. They went as far as to claim that such rock stars as Van Morrison would be attending the event. Of course, this wasn't true, but the *Michigan Daily* picked up the story anyhow. According to the publication 500 people showed up (the police put the number around 150), there were no arrests, and the *Ann Arbor News* called it an "orderly festival."[103]

As a few months went by, an ordinance was drafted by the Ann Arbor City Council making possession of marijuana a small $5 fine, and the Midwestern safe space for cannabis was born.

The very next year, the Hash Bash reported that 5,000 people showed up, including the pro-marijuana legalization State Rep. Perry Bullard, who smiled for the cameras while he was enjoying toking on a joint. As the late '70s and early '80s rolled on, the turnout was less than impressive with it being the "Just Say No" Reagan years, but the Hash Bash refused to die.

The Hash Bash crowd rose up to 5,000 again in 1989, and after some legal pushing and shoving between the University of Michigan and the Michigan chapter of NORML, the Hash Bash was moved to the first Saturday in April in 1991, bringing up to 10,000 cannabis supporters to the Diag.

The Hash Bash just celebrated its 53rd anniversary in 2024. And as always, it is a welcomed tradition after a long, frigid, sometimes not completely over, Michigan winter. The music, the food, the passionate speakers exercising our freedom of speech, and the simple comradery of partaking publicly outdoors is celebrated.

But hear me and heed me, you still must be aware of your steps in Ann Arbor when it comes to possession. You could be on one side of the street and be protected by the Michigan marijuana laws, as you'll be on state/city land. But if you cross that same street and find yourself on campus (federal) property, you are now poking at a very cranky federal bear.[104]

CLOSING

Well, there you have it, folks. You now know what I know about cannabis and how I believe you should apply it to retail. Maybe my stories made you laugh. Maybe they tugged a bit at your heartstrings. But above all, I hope you have learned something that you didn't know before. Some will say this was too much, and others will say that it isn't enough. Both opinions would be correct. We have this very rare opportunity to change the way we approach botanical medicine and take charge of our own healthcare choices.

As I bring this book to a close, I'd be willing to bet that more scientific advances and knowledge about cannabis have been gained since you started reading. For those of us who actually give a shit, the responsibility falls to us not only to keep learning as cannabis research evolves but also to apply that knowledge in a compassionate manner. The beauty of the cannabis culture is ours to lose, and it is my hope that after reading these pages, you will pick up the fight to keep it alive.

GLOSSARY

Bioavailability: "When a substance such as a medicine or supplement enters your system, the portion of the total substance introduces which can effectively create a response determines that substance's bioavailability. The bioavailability of a substance can fluctuate, depending on the route of administration.

Intravenous administration, or a direct line into the bloodstream, is typically considered 100% bioavailability, as all of the substance will reach target cells. In oral administration routes, aka when you take a pill, the amount of medicine or supplement you receive depends on many factors, including your diet and your personal metabolism." https://biologydictionary.net/bioavailability/

Blunt: Cannabis flower rolled up in cigar paper and smoked.

Bong: An apparatus used for smoking cannabis flower with water as a filter. They are generally made from plastic or glass but can be made from dozens of different materials.

Bowl: An apparatus used for smoking flower. They are generally made from glass but can be made from hundreds of different materials.

Burn One: To smoke a joint.

Cannabis: "The word 'cannabis' refers to all products derived from the plant Cannabis sativa" https://www.nccih.nih.gov/health/cannabis-marijuana-and-cannabinoids-what-you-need-to-know

Cannabinoids: "Cannabinoids, broadly speaking, are a class of biological compounds that bind to cannabinoid receptors. They are most frequently sourced from and associated with the plants of the Cannabis genus, including Cannabis sativa, Cannabis indica, and Cannabis ruderalis." Sheikh NK, Dua A. Cannabinoids. [Updated 2023 Feb 27]. In: StatPearls [Internet]. Treasure Island (FL): StatPearls Publishing; 2023 Jan. Available from: https://www.ncbi.nlm.nih.gov/books/NBK556062/

CB1 & CB2 Receptors: "The cannabinoid receptors CB1 and CB2 are key components of the human endocannabinoid system, a biological network involved in regulating physiological and cognitive processes. CB1, which is widely distributed throughout the central nervous system, can be activated by some naturally occurring cannabinoids, or through the use of cannabis and related synthetic compounds, resulting in the 'high' associated with marijuana … CB2 is mainly expressed in the immune system (to a lesser extent in the central nervous system) and does not create a psychotropic reaction." NIDA. 2019, January 25. A whole new view of CB2. Retrieved from https://nida.nih.gov/news-events/news-releases/2019/01/a-whole-new-view-of-cb2 on 2023, May 21

Chemotypes: "… are often defined by the most abundant chemical produced by that individual and the concept has been useful in work done by chemical ecologists and natural product chemists." https://en.wikipedia.org/wiki/Chemotype

COA or Certificate of Analysis: The test results of the cannabis flower that contains total cannabinoid and/or terpene concentrations.

Concentrate: The end product of condensing the cannabis flower.

Other names: Shatter, wax, crumble, badder, resin, rosin, FECO

Cottonmouth: When your mouth is so dry it feels like cotton.

"Cured": The process of removing moisture from a substance. In curing the cannabis plant, trichomes are degraded and therefore less abundant before extraction.

Dab: A hit of concentrate.

Decarboxylation: The process of changing the chemical composition of cannabinoids.

Diamonds/Sand: The end product of crystallized THCA. Diamonds can be crushed to make a sand-like consistency.

Edible: A product that you eat that contains cannabis.

Endocannabinoids: "The endocannabinoid system (ECS) is a widespread neuromodulatory system that plays important roles in central nervous system (CNS) development, synaptic plasticity, and the response to endogenous and environmental insults. The ECS is comprised of cannabinoid receptors, endogenous cannabinoids (endocannabinoids), and the enzymes responsible for the synthesis and degradation of the endocannabinoids." Lu HC, Mackie K. An Introduction to the Endogenous Cannabinoid System. *Biol Psychiatry*. 2016 Apr 1;79(7):516-25. doi: 10.1016/j.biopsych.2015.07.028. Epub 2015 Oct 30. PMID: 26698193; PMCID: PMC4789136.

Flavonoids: "Currently there are about 6000 flavonoids that contribute to the colourful pigments of fruits, herbs, vegetables and medicinal plants." Iwashina T. Contribution to flower colors of flavonoids including anthocyanins: a review. *Nat Prod Commun*. 2015 Mar;10(3):529-44. PMID: 25924543.

FECO: Fully extracted cannabis oil.

Flower: The sticky buds found on the cannabis plant, covered in trichomes that contain cannabinoids, terpenes, and flavonoids.

Other names: Reefer, devil's lettuce, weed, dope, pot, ganja, herb, grass, Mary Jane, Kush, kind, chronic

Negative names: Boof, ditch weed, brick weed, mids, Reggie, schwag, bunk

Genotype: Genotypes are the DNA or blueprint of that particular cannabis plant— its genetic makeup or genetic potential if you will.

Hemp/Industrial Hemp: "Hemp is a botanical class of Cannabis sativa cultivars grown specifically for industrial or medicinal use. It can be used to make a wide range of products. Along with bamboo, hemp is among the fastest-growing plants on Earth. It was also one of the first plants to be spun into usable fiber 50,000 years ago. It can be refined into a variety of commercial items, including paper, rope, textiles, clothing, biodegradable plastics, paint, insulation, biofuel, food, and animal feed." https://en.wikipedia.org/wiki/Hemp

Joint: Cannabis flower rolled up in paper and then smoked like a cigarette.

Other names: Jay, fatty, left-handed cigarette (lefty), doobie

Kief: The trichomes that have been knocked off the cannabis flower. Sometimes collected in the bottom compartment of a flower grinder.

Landrace: A genetically pure cannabis plant.

"Live": Refers to when a cannabis plant is directly flash-frozen at harvest. This preserves more of the trichomes prior to extraction.

Marijuana: "The word marijuana refers to parts of or products from the plant Cannabis sativa that contain substantial amounts of tetrahydrocannabinol (THC)." https://www.nccih.nih.gov/health/cannabis-marijuana-and-cannabinoids-what-you-need-to-know

Moon rocks: A bud rolled in hash oil and then rolled in kief or bubble/ice water hash.

Oil: Can refer to tincture, cartridges, or concentrates.

Phenotype: When a genotype is exposed to the environment (such as temperature, altitude, growing conditions), the result is the plant's phenotype.

Phytocannabinoids: "… a molecule synthesized by plants. There are 113 known phytocannabinoids in the cannabis plant." https://foliumbiosciences.com/what-is-a-phytocannabinoid/

Pen: The battery for vape cartridges or concentrates.

Pinner: A small joint, usually rolled too tight.

Puff, Puff, Pass: A reminder that you are taking too long with your turn when smoking in a group.

Purge: The process of flushing or clearing a cannabis plant of solvents used in the extraction process.

Roach: The remains of a smoked joint.

Rig: An apparatus used for smoking concentrates. It can be heated using a blowtorch or an electric hookup.

RSO: Rick Simpson Oil

Sauce: Liquid terpenes that are added to concentrates for added flavor and effects.

Skins: Rolling papers.

Spliff: A mix of cannabis flower and tobacco rolled up and smoked.

Stepped On: When another substance is added to dilute the original product.

Sublingual: Latin for "under the tongue."

Tarantula Leg: A joint rolled in hash oil and then rolled in kief or bubble/ice water hash.

Terpenes: "... the largest and most diverse group of naturally occurring compounds that are mostly found in plants but larger classes of terpenes such as sterols and squalene can be found in animals. They are responsible for the fragrance, taste, and pigment of plants. The common plant sources of terpenes are tea, thyme, cannabis, Spanish sage, and citrus fruits (e.g., lemon, orange, mandarin)." Cox-Georgian D, Ramadoss N, Dona C, Basu C. Therapeutic and Medicinal Uses of Terpenes. *Medicinal Plants*. 2019 Nov 12:333–59. doi: 10.1007/978- 3-030-31269-5_15. PMCID: PMC7120914.

Tincture: "... a solution of a medicinal substance in an alcoholic solvent." https://www.merriam-webster.com/dictionary/tincture

Total Cannabinoids: The total amount of all of cannabinoids that appear in test results.

Trichomes: "Trichomes are shoot epidermal hairs, found on the majority of plants, and are composed of either single or several cells (Esau, 1977). They play various protective roles, such as being a mechanical barrier to insect herbivores, filtering UV light and reducing respiration." (Fordyce and Agrawal, 2001; Karabourniotis et al., 1992; Levin, 1973; Ripley et al., 1999; Van Dam and Hare,1998).

CORRECTION AND RETRACTION POLICY

I. INTRODUCTION

The integrity of my content is of utmost importance regarding the published *Pot for the People* and the *Budtenders Blueprint*® training. This Correction and Retraction Policy outlines the procedure to address mistakes, inaccuracies, or misleading information that may be discovered in our publications, products, or services.

II. CORRECTIONS

Minor Corrections:

Spelling, Grammar, Punctuation: These corrections will be made promptly without formal notice.

Factual Errors: If a minor factual error is detected, the mistake will be corrected, and a note will be appended to the corrected content, clearly stating the nature and date of the correction.

Major Corrections:

Significant Factual Errors or Misinterpretations: Corrections will be made, and a formal correction notice will be issued alongside the content, clearly explaining the nature and date of the correction.

III. RETRACTIONS

Grounds for Retraction:

Plagiarism

Fraudulent or Fabricated Data

Ethical Misconduct

Retraction Procedure:

Investigation: The issue will be thoroughly investigated by the responsible team or committee.

Decision: A decision to retract will be made in consultation with key stakeholders, such as authors, editors, or legal advisors.

Notification: Affected parties will be notified of the decision.

Public Notice: A retraction notice will be published, clearly stating the reason for retraction and the nature of the offense.

IV. TRANSPARENCY

All corrections and retractions will be handled with full transparency, and all involved parties will be informed as necessary.

V. CONTACT INFORMATION

For questions or to report a concern, please contact:
Angela Roullier
Potforthepeople.co@gmail.com

ENDNOTES

1   https://hashmuseum.com/en/cannabis-knowledge/cannabis-species/

2   https://www.epa.gov/dioxin/learn-about-dioxin

3   https://ecosciences.com/blog/health-and-lifestyle/hemp-can-clean-contaminated-soil/

4   https://www.ncbi.nlm.nih.gov/books/NBK556062/

5   https://www.healthline.com/health/cbd-vs-thc#medical-benefits

6   https://www.projectcbd.org/medicine/dosing-thca-less-more

7   https://www.health.harvard.edu/blog/cannabidiol-cbd-what-we-know-and-what-we-dont-2018082414476

8   https://medical-dictionary.thefreedictionary.com/psychoactive

9   https://www.ncbi.nlm.nih.gov/pmc/articles/PMC8669157/

10   https://www.ncbi.nlm.nih.gov/pmc/articles/PMC8669157/

11   https://www.ncbi.nlm.nih.gov/pmc/articles/PMC8612407/

12   https://www.ncbi.nlm.nih.gov/pmc/articles/PMC8669157/47

13   Walsh KB, McKinney AE, Holmes AE. Minor Cannabinoids: Biosynthesis, Molecular Pharmacology and Potential Therapeutic Uses. *Front Pharmacol*. 2021 Nov 29;12:777804. doi: 10.3389/fphar.2021.777804. PMID: 34916950; PMCID: PMC8669157.

14   Walsh KB, McKinney AE, Holmes AE. Minor Cannabinoids: Biosynthesis, Molecular Pharmacology and Potential Therapeutic Uses. *Front Pharmacol.* 2021 Nov 29;12:777804. doi: 10.3389/fphar.2021.777804. PMID: 34916950; PMCID: PMC8669157.

15   Brierley D. I., Samuels J., Duncan M., Whalley B. J., Williams C. M. (2017). A Cannabigerol-Rich Cannabis Sativa Extract, Devoid of Δ9-tetrahydrocannabinol, Elicits Hyperphagia in Rats. *Behav. Pharmacol.* 28, 280–284. 10.1097/fbp.0000000000000285/

16   https://www.ncbi.nlm.nih.gov/pmc/articles/PMC8669157/

17   https://www.ncbi.nlm.nih.gov/pmc/articles/PMC8669157/

18   https://health.clevelandclinic.org/what-is-delta-8/

19   https://en.wikipedia.org/wiki/Chemotype

20   https://www.researchgate.net/publication/225323012_Time_course_of_cannabinoid_accumulation_and_chemotype_development_during_the_growth_of_Cannabis_sativa_L

21   http://www.TheBigBookofTerps.com

22   https://www.ncbi.nlm.nih.gov/pmc/articles/PMC7120914/

23   https://pubmed.ncbi.nlm.nih.gov/18665271/

24   https://pubmed.ncbi.nlm.nih.gov/31481004/

25   https://www.potforthepeople.co/beta-caryophyllene

26   https://onlinelibrary.wiley.com/doi/abs/10.1002/ptr.2247

27   https://pubmed.ncbi.nlm.nih.gov/17559833/

28   https://pubmed.ncbi.nlm.nih.gov/18665271/

29   https://pubmed.ncbi.nlm.nih.gov/31481004/

30   https://www.potforthepeople.co/beta-caryophyllene

31   https://www.ncbi.nlm.nih.gov/pmc/articles/PMC6007527/

32   https://www.ncbi.nlm.nih.gov/pmc/articles/PMC8326332/

33   https://www.ncbi.nlm.nih.gov/pmc/articles/PMC6920849/

34   https://www.ncbi.nlm.nih.gov/pmc/articles/PMC4329611/

35   https://www.ncbi.nlm.nih.gov/pmc/articles/PMC5465813/

36   https://www.sciencedirect.com/science/article/abs/pii/B9780123858511000044

37   https://www.accesswire.com/473598/Industry-Pioneer-David-Watson-Joins-United-Cannabis-Corp-Advisory-Board

38   https://www.fastcompany.com/48172/dr-dopes-connection

39   https://biologydictionary.net/bioavailability/

40   https://www.veriheal.com/blog/cannabinoid-boiling-points-a-guide-to-optimal-vaporizer-temperatures/

41   https://flowhub.com/learn/top-selling-cannabis-products

42   Medicinal Cannabis: In Vitro Validation of Vaporizers for the Smoke-Free Inhalation of Cannabis - PMC (nih.gov)

43   https://druglibrary.org/MedicalMj/hash/history_of_hashish.htm

44   https://www.drugs.com/illicit/hashish.html

45   https://www.frenchydreamsofhashish.com/

46   https://www.britannica.com/science/carbon-dioxide

47   https://www.extractz.com/what-is-co2-extraction

48   https://medium.com/@Z_Lucie/cannabis-extractions-the-complete-guide-151edb382d65

49   https://terpenesandtesting.com/butane-extraction-101/

50   https://extraktlab.com/thca-diamonds/

51   https://enviroprod.com/blogs/news/what-is-food-grade-alcohol

52   https://sciencing.com/naphtha-uses-7665916.html

53   https://keytocannabis.com/low-temp-dabs-vs-high-the-perfect-temperature-for-dab-potency-and-flavor/

54   https://pubmed.ncbi.nlm.nih.gov/4729039/

55   https://www.mayoclinic.org/tests-procedures/cyp450-test/about/pac-20393711

56   https://pubmed.ncbi.nlm.nih.gov/26651971/

57   Human Cannabinoid Pharmacokinetics - PMC (nih.gov)

58   A Systematic Review on the Pharmacokinetics of Cannabidiol in Humans - PMC (nih.gov)

59   https://www.ncbi.nlm.nih.gov/pmc/articles/PMC4403087/

60   https://pubmed.ncbi.nlm.nih.gov/26517407/

61   https://www.ncbi.nlm.nih.gov/pmc/articles/PMC6

62   https://www.potforthepeople.co/skin-conditions

63   https://www.ncbi.nlm.nih.gov/pmc/articles/PMC6222489/

64   https://pmc.ncbi.nlm.nih.gov/articles/PMC8489354/

65   https://en.wikipedia.org/wiki/ADME

66   https://www.healthline.com/nutrition/oranges#nutrition

67   https://www.medicalnewstoday.com/articles/full-spectrum-cbd-vs-broad-spectrum-cbd#differences

68   https://www.scirp.org/pdf/PP_2015021016351567.pdf

69   https://www.mlive.com/public-interest/2022/03/marijuana-regulators-consider-notifying-consumers-if-their-product-failed-testing.html

70   Crocq MA. History of cannabis and the endocannabinoid system. *Dialogues Clin Neurosci.* 2020 Sep;22(3):223-228. doi: 10.31887/DCNS.2020.22.3/mcrocq. PMID: 33162765; PMCID: PMC7605027

71   https://www.health.harvard.edu/blog/the-endocannabinoid-system-essential-and-mysterious-202108112569

72   https://terpenesandtesting.com/category/science/cannabis-allergies/

73   Galli JA, Sawaya RA, Friedenberg FK. Cannabinoid hyperemesis syndrome. *Curr Drug Abuse Rev.* 2011 Dec;4(4):241-9. doi: 10.2174/1874473711104040241. PMID:

22150623; PMCID: PMC3576702

74   https://www.frontiersin.org/journals/toxicology/articles/10.3389/ftox.2024.1465728/full

75   https://www.frontiersin.org/journals/toxicology/articles/10.3389/ftox.2024.1465728/full

76   https://www.drugs.com/article/grapefruit-drug-interactions.html

77   https://www.usdrugtestcenters.com/drug-test-blog/181/can-you-fail-a-drug-test-due-to-cbd.html

78   https://www.medicalnewstoday.com/articles/324315#failing-a-drug-test

79   https://medical-dictionary.thefreedictionary.com/static+ataxia

80   https://www.ncbi.nlm.nih.gov/pmc/articles/PMC6770351/

81   https://pubmed.ncbi.nlm.nih.gov/32118071/

82   De Briyne N, Holmes D, Sandler I, Stiles E, Szymanski D, Moody S, Neumann S, Anadon A. Cannabis, Cannabidiol Oils and Tetrahydrocannabinol-What Do Veterinarians Need to Know? *Animals* (Basel). 2021 Mar 20;11(3):892. doi: 10.3390/ani11030892. PMID: 33804793; PMCID: PMC8003882.

83   https://www.nccih.nih.gov/health/cannabis-marijuana-and-cannabinoids-what-you-need-to-know

84   https://www.history.com/news/the-hazy-history-of-420

85   https://sports.yahoo.com/news/tiger-stadium-opened-100-years-ago-just-like-fenway-park--but-it-s-ignored-in-detroit.html

86   https://www.history.com/news/the-hazy-history-of-420

87   https://www.jackherer.com/

88   https://en.wikipedia.org/wiki/Jack_Herer#cite_note-2

89   https://nida.nih.gov/publications/research-reports/marijuana/what-are-effects-secondhand-exposure-to-marijuana-smoke on 2023, March 16

90   https://www.wikileaf.com/thestash/rick-simpson-oil/

91   Uekotter, Frank. The Revolt of the Chemists: biofuels, agricultural overproduction and the chemurgy movement in New Deal America History and Technology, 37:4, pg. 431

Pursell, Carroll W. The Farm Chemurgic Council and the United States Department of Agriculture, 1935-1939 *Isis*, Vol. 60 No. 3 Autumn 1969 pg. 310

Ibid; 309

Uekotter, Frank. The Revolt of the Chemists: biofuels, agricultural overproduction and the chemurgy movement in New Deal America. *History and Technology*, 37:4, pp. 435-436

Van Duyne, Schulyer. Henry Ford Demonstrates Plastic Bodies for Cars. *Popular Science*. March 1941

Harris, Kathryn. New Book on Henry Ford Libel Trial Sheds Light on History of Hate Speech. https://www.americanbarfoundation.org/news/345 June 14, 2012 accessed March 8, 2023

92   https://www.higherlearninglv.co/post/the-higher-learning-lv-interview-richard-rose

93   https://therichardrosereport.com/1994-hempeh-burger/

94   https://therichardrosereport.com/articles2/richard-rose-professional-history/

95   https://therichardrosereport.com/about/

96   https://hemptoday.net/richard-rose-interview/

97   https://cannigma.com/physiology/foods-that-can-affect-your-high/

98   https://cannigma.com/cannabis-news/does-holding-cannabis-smoke-in-longer-make-a-difference/

99   https://www.globaldrugsurvey.com/wp-content/themes/globaldrugsurvey/results/GDS2017_key-findings-report_final.pdf

100   https://cannigma.com/research/wake-and-bake/

101   https://cannabis.net/blog/opinion/cannabis-urban-legend-the-white-ash-vs.-black-ash-myth

102   https://www.veriheal.com/blog/growing-cannabis/why-turn-purple/

103   https://komornlaw.com/some-hash-bash-history/

104   https://dpss.umich.edu/content/prevention-education/safety-tips/alcohol-drugs/marijuana-u-m-faq/